ENGAGE

The Art of Spiritual Warfare

SEYI OLADOSU

Engage: The Art of Spiritual Warfare

Copyright © 2024, Seyi Oladosu. All rights reserved.

The author has asserted his right to be identified as the author of this work in accordance with the Copyright, Designs, and Patents Act 1988.

No part of this publication may be reproduced, stored in a retrieval system, or transmitted, in any form or by any means, electronic, mechanical, photocopying, recording, or otherwise, without the prior permission of the author.

All scripture quotations, unless otherwise indicated, are taken from the Holy Bible, King James Version, Cambridge University Press, Oxford University Press, HarperCollins and the Queen's Printers.

Published in the United Kingdom by Seyi Oladosu Publishing

ISBN: 978-1-7392146-8-5

DEDICATION

By the grace of God, this book is dedicated to my grand-dad of blessed memories Pa Joshua Oladosu, a man of prayer and a great lover of God, he was an assistant Pastor in his local assembly; To all my prayer partners, genuine prayer warriors, and people sharpened and shaped through adversarial situations.

Victory on every side.

Arise and Shine!

CONTENTS

Acknowledgement 7

Introduction 9

1. The Battlefield 11
2. The Battle Life 21
3. The Battle Plan 29
4. The Battle Gate 39
5. How to Engage 49
6. When to Engage 59
7. Guaranteed Victory 67
8. Possessing Your Possession 83
9. Overcoming Negative Thoughts 91
10. Taking Authority 99
11. Confident Living 125

ACKNOWLEDGEMENT

Glory, honour, and praise be to the Almighty God for making it possible for this book to come forth. With God, nothing is impossible. To Him be all the glory forever.

To my beloved Dad and Mum, Bishop I. F. and Lady E. A. Oladosu, your lifestyle of prayer, most essentially spiritual warfare, impacted and imparted my life growing up till now. It's always glorious and priceless to have praying parents. Memories of those early morning and nightfall prayer times still linger. Psalm 3 has been a phenomenal, peculiar, and unforgettable experience till date.

To my friend, Yomi Opoola, your insatiable thirst for prayer encouraged me a lot. I am so eternally grateful that you pulled me into the prayer department during our Youth Service.

Also, I sincerely appreciate all your beautiful efforts, Pastor Fatai Kasali, for ensuring this book was delivered excellently and promptly. You are a genuine helper of destiny. Blessed forever.

A big well done to man of impact, Pastor James Adeyemi for all the brilliant creative designs.

To all members of TPL, thank you.

Praise God for my family.

What would have been done without you, my beautiful wife, and children? Thank God for your awesome gift of kindness, laughter, gentle push, whispers of encouragement, pleasant reminders, and particularly for inventing the space to get the job done. I so much appreciate God in you.

INTRODUCTION

If it had not been for the Lord on our side, we would have been completely removed.

Being indomitable is not by power nor by might but by the Spirit of the Lord.

God's mercies never fail; they are new every morning.

Life is not a funfair but warfare. We are on a battlefield.

There is always a battle between light and darkness, between good and evil.

Every soldier that is on battlefield of life, therefore, does not entangle themselves with the affairs of this world so that they might please the one who has chosen them to be soldiers.

However, there is wisdom and order in spiritual warfare. Christian believers are soldiers of the Lord, and the Lord is the Commander-in-Chief of all armed forces, i.e., the Commander of the heavenly battalions. God can fight on the land, on the sea, in the air, under the sea, and everywhere and anywhere. He can overrule but cannot be overruled. He is higher than the highest and greater than the greatest. He formed everything. He created the smith that brought forth instruments. He created the waster to destroy. No weapon formed against you shall prosper. Tongues risen against you in judgement are condemned in Jesus' name.

2 Corinthians 10:3-5

For although we live in the natural realm, we don't wage a military campaign employing human weapons, using manipulation to achieve our aims.

Instead, our spiritual weapons are energised with divine power to effectively dismantle the defenses behind which people hide.

We can demolish every deceptive fantasy that opposes God and break through every arrogant attitude that is raised up in defiance of the true knowledge of God. We capture, like prisoners of war, every thought and insist that it bow in obedience to the Anointed One.

Every army of hell is pulled down because they pull down good things being built. Their mission statement to steal, kill, and destroy is hereby terminated, abolished, and destroyed in Jesus' name.

No army can block our way. We are the army of the sovereign God. Our army cannot be stopped; we belong to God.

No demon can block our way because we have Jesus' name.

No devil can block our way because we have Jesus' blood.

No weapon can block our way because we have Jesus' word.

No sickness can block our way because we have Jesus' stripes.

No mountain can block our way because we have Jesus' faith.

Arise, soldiers of the Lord! Arise and shout. Hallelujah!

I see you win the battles of life against visible and invisible forces, external and internal powers, in Jesus' name.

Regret looks back. Fear looks around. Worry looks in. Faith looks up.

Be strong in the Lord and in the power of His might…Put on the whole armour of God to be able to stand against the wiles of the devil… Our wrestle is not against flesh and blood but against principalities, against powers, against the rulers of darkness of this world and against spiritual wickedness in heavenly places…Take unto you therefore the whole armour of God that you may be able to stand in the evil day, and having done all to stand.

Stand therefore…

Chapter 1

THE BATTLEFIELD

1 Timothy 6:12
Fight the good fight of faith, lay hold on eternal life, whereunto thou art also called, and hast professed a good profession before many witnesses.

To ENGAGE means:

Combat, encounter, launch, strike, do battle with, fall on, give battle to, join battle with, take on.

- Battle is the seed for taking territories.

The spiritual world actually exists. Life is not a funfair or jamboree but a battlefield.

- As Christians, we have a mandate to confront the devil.

Luke 10:17-19
Then the seventy returned with joy, saying, "Lord, even the demons are subject to us in Your name." And He said to them, "I saw Satan fall like lightning from heaven. Behold, I give you the authority to trample on serpents and scorpions, and over all the power of the enemy, and nothing shall by any means hurt you.

- Mandate to cast out devils.

MARK 16:17
And these signs will follow those who believe: In My name they will cast out demons; they will speak with new tongues

- Anytime God says I can do something, there is enough power in His word to enable me to do what He says.

Because there is no impossibility with God, no word of the Lord shall be impossible.

LUKE 1:37
For with God nothing shall be impossible.

MARK 11:23-24
For verily I say unto you, That whosoever shall say unto this mountain, Be thou removed, and be thou cast into the sea; and shall not doubt in his heart, but shall believe that those things which he saith shall come to pass; he shall have whatsoever he saith. Therefore I say unto you, What things soever ye desire, when ye pray, believe that ye receive them, and ye shall have them.

ISAIAH 55:11
So shall my word be that goeth forth out of my mouth: it shall not return unto me void, but it shall accomplish that which I please, and it shall prosper in the thing whereto I sent it.

NUMBERS 23:19
God is not a man, that he should lie; Neither the son of man, that he should repent: Hath he said, and shall he not do it? Or hath he spoken, and shall he not make it good?

- Whatever God says, He empowers (Delegated Authority).

Hence, we walk in spiritual authority when we cast out devils.

COLOSSIANS 1:16
For by Him were all things created, that are in heaven, and that are in earth, visible and invisible...

- We can't see spiritual arenas with physical eyes, and we should know that the spiritual world affects the physical earth.

2 Corinthians 2:11
Paul reminds us: "lest Satan should take advantage of us. For we are not ignorant of his devices."
We are not ignorant of devices, schemes, and intentions of Satan.

- Satan uses people, demonic spirits, situations, and thoughts as weapons. Many people are facing spiritual struggles as they attempt to advance in the things of God. One of the primary tricks of the enemy is to get a person deceived and not realising the depth of what is taking place in their lives.

Oftentimes people assume that the struggle they are facing is just a natural battle yet just beneath the surface there is something far more complex taking place. They are under a spiritual attack!

If you're advancing the kingdom of God in some capacity, you can bet you will come up spiritual attacks.

A spiritual attack is a series of events coordinated by the demonic realm in order to abort promises, shipwreck faith, oppress a believer and stall out destiny.

The Bible tells us that the devil has various plots and schemes he uses against human beings. Many people wrongly assume that Satan is stupid, yet he has been studying the thoughts, actions and behaviour of humanity since the beginning of time. He knows how to tempt people.

He masters at pushing the right buttons at the right time! We must not be ignorant to the strategies of the enemy. We can not live our lives with our spiritual eyes shut. We must walk in the spirit and be aware of what is taking place around us.

Knowing there's an assault against you.

When you're QUESTIONING God's word and His goodness and doubting.

Genesis 3:6-7, 12
So when the woman saw that the tree was good for food, that it was pleasant to the eyes, and a tree desirable to make one wise, she took of its fruit and ate. She also gave to her husband with her, and he ate. Then the eyes of both of them were opened, and they knew that they were naked; and they sewed fig leaves together and made themselves coverings. Then the man said, "The woman whom You gave to be with me, she gave me of the tree, and I ate."

When you are LUKEWARM, unstable, and no longer active as you used to be. When you're fainting and weary and no longer fervent.

Revelation 3:16
So then, because you are lukewarm and neither cold nor hot, I will vomit you out of My mouth.

When WRONG THINGS BECOME MORE ATTRACTIVE than the right things in your choices.

James 1:14
But each one is tempted when he is drawn away by his own desires and enticed.

Focusing on our problems, WORRYING RATHER THAN LOOKING UNTO GOD. Exalting our problems to be bigger than God.

2 Corinthians 4:18
While we do not look at the things which are seen, but at the things which are not seen. For the things which are seen are temporary, but the things which are not seen are eternal.

Philippians 4:6
Be anxious for nothing, but in everything by prayer and supplication, with thanksgiving, let your requests be made known to God;

Why ENGAGE?

To thwart Satan's desire and agenda to be God and ACCUSE the brethren {embarrassing God} and impose his will on the earth {contrary to God's will}.

Isaiah 14:14
I will ascend above the heights of the clouds, I will be like the Most High.'

Because of his desire to ERADICATE you from God, he wants you missing in action by all means.

Daniel 7:25
He shall speak pompous words against the Most High, Shall persecute the saints of the Most High, And shall intend to change times and law. Then the saints shall be given into his hand For a time and times and half a time.

Because of his desire to TORMENT & TERRORISE all those made in the image of God, whether born again or not.

John 10:10
The thief does not come except to steal, and to kill, and to destroy. I have come that they may have life, and that they may have it more abundantly.

Because of his desire to DECEIVE us concerning things of God, entice, misinform, and give us suggestive thoughts that are not in line with the word of God.

Revelation 20:3
And cast him into the bottomless pit, and shut him up, and set a seal upon him, that he should deceive the nations no more, till the thousand years should be fulfilled: and after that he must be loosed a little season.

Because of his desire to CONFUSE people with depression and spiritual blindness.

2 Corinthians 4:3-4
But even if our gospel is veiled, it is veiled to those who are perishing, whose minds the god of this age has blinded, who do not believe, lest the light of the gospel of the glory of Christ, who is the image of God, should shine on them.

Because of his desire to ABORT every prophetic word of God from being fulfilled.

1 Thessalonians 2:18
Therefore we wanted to come to you—even I, Paul, time and again—but Satan hindered us.

To RECLAIM all lost and stolen territories back, overthrow all satanic hold and lordship, and enforce the mandate of God.

Ezekiel 21:25-27
'Now to you, O profane, wicked prince of Israel, whose day has come, whose iniquity shall end, thus says the Lord God: "Remove the turban, and take off the crown; Nothing shall remain the same. Exalt the humble, and humble the exalted. Overthrown, overthrown, I will make it overthrown! It shall be no longer, Until He comes whose right it is, And I will give it to Him."'

Satanic Infiltration

- warning signs

Satan loves to pull Christians into unhealthy extremes.

Many immature Christian leaders sometimes allow youthful pride, greed or insecurity to suck them into toxic spirituality. The result is always a trail of wounded people.

The Warning Signs

1. No Accountability

Healthy leaders know they need to surround themselves with mentors and advisers who can question them if they step out of line.

Proverbs 11:14
In the multitude of counsellors there is safety.

If you are following a teacher, prophet or apostle who has not submitted himself to any form of accountability, you are asking for trouble. Never align yourself with a Lone Ranger, no matter how fiery his sermons are. He will likely lead you off a cliff.

2. Love of Money.

Godly leaders always call people to fund the work of the gospel; unhealthy leaders, on the contrary, manipulate people in order to line their own pockets. Don't be charmed when a preacher makes outlandish promises about what will happen if you give to him.

1 Timothy 6:10
For the love of money is a root of all kinds of evil, for which some have strayed from the faith in their greediness, and pierced themselves through with many sorrows.

Hebrew 13:5
Let your conduct be without covetousness; be content with such things as you have. For He Himself has said, "I will never leave you nor forsake you."

3. A Prideful Cultist

Many Christians who experience certain gifts or manifestations of the Holy Spirit are sometimes tempted to think they are superior, this subtle spiritual pride can lead into formation of a dangerous cultist group. Don't let anyone suck you into this kind of cultic mindset.

1 Timothy 4:1-2
Now the Spirit expressly says that in latter times some will depart from the faith, giving heed to deceiving spirits and doctrines of demons, speaking lies in hypocrisy, having their own conscience seared with a hot iron.

4. A Controlling Oppressive Spirit

Insecure and untrained leaders use manipulation and threats to keep their followers loyal. Oppressive leaders constantly emphasises control, demanding total submission. This mindset can lead to serious spiritual abuse.

1 Peter 5:2-3
Shepherd the flock of God which is among you, serving as overseers, not by compulsion but willingly, not for dishonest gain but eagerly; nor as being Lords over those entrusted to you, but being examples to the flock.

5. False Miracles

There's a deep hunger in the body of Christ for healing, prophecy and the full manifestation of the Holy Spirit's power. In the quest to see

God's power displayed, some people fall into the trap of hyping, faking miracles to get attention.

2 Thessalonians 2:9
The coming of the lawless one is according to the working of Satan, with all power, signs, and lying wonders.

Matthew 24:24
For false christs and false prophets will rise and show great signs and wonders to deceive, if possible, even the elect.

6. False Doctrines

The apostle Paul warned us long ago that waves of deception would affect the church.

2 Timothy 4:3-4
For the time will come when people will no longer endure sound doctrine... they will turn their ears away from the truth...

If something sounds really off when you hear it, don't ignore your gut feelings. Don't be deceived. Discern the moment. Every genuine Christian is equipped with an intuition system that will warn you about any unhealthy teaching or ministry.

7. Unhealthy Rivalry

When Christian groups compete against each other, and ministries fight for their turf, the enemy is winning. Internal fighting destroys church from within.

1 Corinthians 1:10
Now I plead with you, brethren, by the name of our Lord Jesus Christ, that you all speak the same thing, and that there be no divisions among you, but that you be perfectly joined together in the same mind and in the same judgment.

8. Immaturity Among Believers

When leaders are still essentially baby believers, the door is open for Satan's forces. Carnalities, secularism and works of the flesh will still be in mighty display.

1 Corinthians 3:3
For you are still carnal. For where there are envy, strife, and divisions among you, are you not carnal and behaving like mere men?

9. Internal Strife

The Corinthians apparently regularly filed grievances against one another rather than try to work them out in Christian love. Internal strife marked their congregation.

1 Corinthians 6:6
But brother goes to law against brother, and that before unbelievers!

10. Sexual Immorality in the Church

Paul so often spoke against sexual sin and called believing couples to give themselves to each other physically lest Satan tempt them. This problem is real, powerful and prevalent in many churches of today. Tolerating sin in the congregation.

The Corinthians not only knew about open sin in the church, but they also boasted about it, ignoring sin is evidence of Satan's influence.

1 Corinthians 10:8
Nor let us commit sexual immorality, as some of them did, and in one day twenty-three thousand fell.

1 Corinthians 5:1
It is actually reported that there is sexual immorality among you, and such sexual immorality as is not even named among the Gentiles—that a man has his father's wife!

11. Misuse of Christian Liberty

Living in our freedom without regard for others—and the enemy finds working room when we're self-centered.

1 Corinthians 8:9
But beware lest somehow this liberty of yours become a stumbling block to those who are weak.

12. Idolatry

The demons delight when we elevate someone, something, or some action above the true God.

1 Corinthians 10:14
Therefore, my beloved, flee from idolatry.

13. Unwillingness to Forgive a Repentant Believer

When we don't forgive and restore a repentant brother or sister in Christ, we open the door to the enemy's influence and the enemy sows falsehood.

2 Corinthians 2:6-7, 11
This punishment which was inflicted by the majority is sufficient for such a man, so that, on the contrary, you ought rather to forgive and comfort him, lest perhaps such a one be swallowed up with too much sorrow... lest Satan should take advantage of us; for we are not ignorant of his devices.

Chapter 2

THE BATTLE LIFE

Ephesians 6:12
For we wrestle not against flesh and blood, but against principalities, against powers, against the rulers of the darkness of this world, against spiritual wickedness in high places.

2 Timothy 2:1-4
You therefore, my son, be strong in the grace that is in Christ Jesus. And the things that you have heard from me among many witnesses, commit these to faithful men who will be able to teach others also. You therefore must endure hardship as a good soldier of Jesus Christ. No one engaged in warfare entangles himself with the affairs of this life, that he may please him who enlisted him as a soldier.

Soldiers are ENGAGERS. They are true, loyal, brave, good, duty-bound, enlisted, and drafted by Jesus Christ.

Rules of Engagement

{For Soldiers}

They're rugged, so they endure, permit, tolerate, and withstand hardness.

Because of the nature of their assignment, they are neither complainers nor slothful. They expect the ruggedness and endurance as part of their lives.

1 Peter 3:17
For it is better, if it is the will of God, to suffer for doing good than for doing evil.

2 Corinthians 11:23-28
Are they ministers of Christ?—I speak as a fool—I am more: in labors more abundant, in stripes above measure, in prisons more frequently, in deaths often. From the Jews five times I received forty stripes minus one. Three times I was beaten with rods; once I was stoned; three times I was shipwrecked; a night and a day I have been in the deep; in journeys often, in perils of waters, in perils of robbers, in perils of my own countrymen, in perils of the Gentiles, in perils in the city, in perils in the wilderness, in perils in the sea, in perils among false brethren; in weariness and toil, in sleeplessness often, in hunger and thirst, in fastings often, in cold and nakedness— besides the other things, what comes upon me daily: my deep concern for all the churches.

They never give up. The ruggedness comes with the profile.

A soldier never involves himself or gets wrapped up or mixed up with the affairs of the world.

They avoid distractions to be able to focus on the commander-in-chief and the assignment.

1 John 2:15-17
Do not love the world or the things in the world. If anyone loves the world, the love of the Father is not in him. For all that is in the world—the lust of the flesh, the lust of the eyes, and the pride of life—is not of the Father but is of the world. And the world is passing away, and the lust of it; but he who does the will of God abides forever.

They avoid things that mess up with their disciplines. Does not entangle so as not to weaken them and the calling.

They are well-trained.

Taught, tough and learned. They're relied on to perform. They're made ready, sharpened, and shaped. They are better trained and effective. They maintain a disciplined lifestyle and prepare for even psychological warfare.

PSALM 144:1
Blessed be the Lord my Rock, Who trains my hands for war, And my fingers for battle.

They are well dressed.

They are neat, clean, and wear protective clothing. They wear the armour of God. {Break down one by one and explain for study purposes}.

- Helmet of Salvation
- Breastplate of Righteousness
- Girdle or belt of Truth
- Shield of Faith
- Sandals of gospel of Peace
- Sword of the Spirit {which is the Word of God}
- Praying in the Spirit

EPHESIANS 6:14-18
Stand therefore, having girded your waist with truth, having put on the breastplate of righteousness, and having shod your feet with the preparation of the gospel of peace; above all, taking the shield of faith with which you will be able to quench all the fiery darts of the wicked one. And take the helmet of salvation, and the sword of the Spirit, which is the word of God; praying always with all prayer and supplication in the Spirit, being watchful to this end with all perseverance and supplication for all the saints.

They are obedient to authority.

Order is always given to engage. Command is issued to engage. Engage with voices in your head, conflicts in your mind, sin, lust, critics, doubt, negative thoughts, and impossibilities.

2 Corinthians 10:4-5
For the weapons of our warfare are not carnal but mighty in God for pulling down strongholds... casting down arguments and every high thing that exalts itself against the knowledge of God, bringing every thought into captivity to the obedience of Christ.

They are loyal.

They are faithful to the cause, leadership, government, obligation, oath, total allegiance, patriotic, devoted, dutiful, steadfast, and trustworthy.

2 Timothy 2:4
No one engaged in warfare entangles himself with the affairs of this life, that he may please him who enlisted him as a soldier.

Reasons to be Strong

Engagement is for improvement, for a better nation, companies, and churches. Make efforts to change things for the better, and take the battle to the gate.

1. Commanded by God

Ephesians 6:10
Finally, my brethren, be strong in the Lord and in the power of His might.

Ezekiel 3:8
Behold, I have made thy face strong against their faces, and thy forehead strong against their foreheads.

2. To Resist and Push Down and Flush Out Enemies

Ward off opposition, hatred, adversaries, fear, ailment, infirmities, and barriers.

James 4:7
Therefore submit to God. Resist the devil and he will flee from you.

I Peter 5:8-9
Be sober, be vigilant; because your adversary the devil walks about like a roaring lion, seeking whom he may devour. Resist him, steadfast in the faith, knowing that the same sufferings are experienced by your brotherhood in the world.

3. We Engage to Keep What We Have

Our influence, position, possessions, family, good name, righteousness, ministry, health, joy, peace, intellect, prosperity etc.

Ephesians 4:27
Nor give place to the devil.

4. To Go Forward: Advance and Make Progress

Dethrone illegal occupants, take new territories and recover lost or stolen territories.

Exodus 23:30
Little by little I will drive them out from before you, until you have increased, and you inherit the land. To fight for the Spiritually immature, the weak, children in the family, babes in Christ, brethren, and the vulnerable. Those who can't normally or generally fight for themselves.

Nehemiah 4:14
And I looked, and arose and said to the nobles, to the leaders, and to the rest of the people, "Do not be afraid of them. Remember the Lord, great and awesome, and fight for your brethren, your sons, your daughters, your wives, and your houses."

Joshua 1:9
Have I not commanded you? Be strong and of good courage; do not be afraid, nor be dismayed, for the Lord your God is with you wherever you go.

6. Because There is No Other Way Out – No More Options

There are stubborn pursuers and wicked spirits. No retreat and no surrender.

Exodus 14:13-15

And Moses said to the people, "Do not be afraid. Stand still, and see the salvation of the Lord, which He will accomplish for you today. For the Egyptians whom you see today, you shall see again no more forever. The Lord will fight for you, and you shall hold your peace." And the Lord said to Moses, "Why do you cry to Me? Tell the children of Israel to go forward.

2 Chronicles 20:22-24

Now when they began to sing and to praise, the Lord set ambushes against the people of Ammon, Moab, and Mount Seir, who had come against Judah; and they were defeated. For the people of Ammon and Moab stood up against the inhabitants of Mount Seir to utterly kill and destroy them. And when they had made an end of the inhabitants of Seir, they helped to destroy one another. So when Judah came to a place overlooking the wilderness, they looked toward the multitude; and there were their dead bodies, fallen on the earth. No one had escaped.

7. Because of the Nature of the Assignment

Your adversary is not weak. Strength is important. Through God we shall do valiantly and our enemies shall be subdued and crushed. Greater is He that lives in us. When God is with us, who can be against us.

Isaiah 40:29-31

He gives power to the weak, And to those who have no might He increases strength. Even the youths shall faint and be weary, And the young men shall utterly fall, But those who wait on the Lord Shall renew their strength; They shall mount up with wings like eagles, They shall run and not be weary, They shall walk and not faint.

2 Timothy 2:1

You therefore, my son, be strong in the grace that is in Christ Jesus.

8. Because of the Realm of Warfare

The realm of the spirit is a place of warfare. Battles of life are won not in the physical realm but first in the spiritual realm because there are spiritual wickedness in heavenly places. Prince of Persia, territorial spirits, guardian gods, power in the air must be defeated and destroyed.

2 Corinthians 10:3
For though we walk in the flesh, we do not war according to the flesh.

Ephesians 6:12
For we do not wrestle against flesh and blood, but against principalities, against powers, against the rulers of the darkness of this age, against spiritual hosts of wickedness in the heavenly places.

1 Corinthians 15:32
If, in the manner of men, I have fought with beasts at Ephesus, what advantage is it to me? If the dead do not rise, "Let us eat and drink, for tomorrow we die!"

Chapter 3

THE BATTLE PLAN

1 Timothy 6:12
Fight the good fight of faith, lay hold on eternal life, to which you were also called and have confessed the good confession in the presence of many witnesses.

1 John 4:4
You are of God, little children, and have overcome them, because He who is in you is greater than he who is in the world.

Every soldier of Christ is God's frontline assault force.

You have an enemy who is doing his dead-level best to destroy you. In this crucial, all-out, no-holds-barred offensive, Satan will dispatch hell's choicest personnel to bring you down.

If you're going to make it through in victory, you NEED to put yourself in training as an overcomer.

You must be unreasonably committed, obtain wisdom, and get understanding.

To be able to formulate a well-orchestrated divine plan or layout for battle, we need to consider the following:

The extent to which I know the truth is the extent to which I can function effectively in spiritual warfare. Spiritual maturity is necessary.

Saturation of revelation is crucial. Be soaked and sanctified with the truth of God's word. Rooted and grounded in the word.

JOHN 8:31-32
Then Jesus said to those Jews who believed Him, "If you abide in My word, you are My disciples indeed. And you shall know the truth, and the truth shall make you free."

Certain levels of spiritual maturity are required to deal with Satan. It is God's will to be delivered, so we must persevere to cast out devils.

MARK 9:20-27 {DEAF & DUMB SPIRIT CAST OUT}
Then they brought him to Him. And when he saw Him, immediately the spirit convulsed him, and he fell on the ground and wallowed, foaming at the mouth. So He asked his father, "How long has this been happening to him?" And he said, "From childhood. And often he has thrown him both into the fire and into the water to destroy him. But if You can do anything, have compassion on us and help us." When Jesus saw that the people came running together, He rebuked the unclean spirit, saying to it: "Deaf and dumb spirit, I command you, come out of him and enter him no more!"

But Jesus took him by the hand and lifted him up, and he arose.

Satanic encroachment & deception lead to death, as in Ananias and Sapphira.

ACTS 5:1-4
But a certain man named Ananias, with Sapphira his wife, sold a possession. And he kept back part of the proceeds, his wife also being aware of it, and brought a certain part and laid it at the apostles' feet. But Peter said, "Ananias, why has Satan filled your heart to lie to the Holy Spirit and keep back part of the price of the land for yourself? While it remained, was it not your own? And after it was sold, was it not in your own control? Why have you conceived this thing in your heart? You have not lied to men but to God."

When we are attacked, we must respond with the word of God because spiritually mature people are not immune to satanic attacks.

In MATT. 4:1-11, Jesus, after 40 days of fasting and prayer, was led to the wilderness to be tempted by the devil.

Then Jesus was led up by the Spirit into the wilderness to be tempted by the devil... Then Jesus said to him, "Away with you, Satan! For it is written, 'You shall worship the Lord your God, and Him only you shall serve.'" Then the devil left Him, and behold, angels came and ministered to Him.

People with no relationship with God have no power or authority over Satan.

ACTS 19:13-16 {SONS OF SCEVA}
Then some of the itinerant Jewish exorcists took it upon themselves to call the name of the Lord Jesus over those who had evil spirits, saying, "We exorcise you by the Jesus whom Paul preaches." Also there were seven sons of Sceva, a Jewish chief priest, who did so. And the evil spirit answered and said, "Jesus I know, and Paul I know; but who are you?" Then the man in whom the evil spirit was, leaped on them, overpowered them, and prevailed against them, so that they fled out of that house naked and wounded.

We are sealed with the Holy Spirit. There is a stamp or seal of God on us, so demons tremble and fear when they see you as a believer. You no longer have to fear as you've been authorised to cast out devils.

EPHESIANS 1:13
In Him you also trusted, after you heard the word of truth, the gospel of your salvation; in whom also, having believed, you were sealed with the Holy Spirit of promise...

GALATIANS 6:17
From now on let no one trouble me, for I bear in my body the marks of the Lord Jesus.

The devil runs & flees from the authority in the name of Jesus you represent, and that is in you.

1 JOHN 4:4
You are of God, little children, and have overcome them, because He who is in you is greater than he who is in the world.

Appreciate the power in the name of Jesus because we've been authorised to police the earth in the spirit realm. Whatever the devil is behind or involved in must bow at the name of Jesus. The name must be used as if Jesus were physically present.

Philippians 2:9-11
Therefore God also has highly exalted Him and given Him the name which is above every name, that at the name of Jesus every knee should bow, of those in heaven, and of those on earth, and of those under the earth, and that every tongue should confess that Jesus Christ is Lord, to the glory of God the Father.

Principles to Guide for Battle Plan

Principle of Salvation

To engage in battle with unseen forces, spiritual wickedness, and cohorts, you must be born again. Through salvation we become partakers of divine inheritance, we are enlisted into the army of the Lord and the enjoy the divine back up of our defender, for our God is the commander in chief of the heavenly forces, the Lord of host, the Lord strong and mighty in battle, the man of war

John 3:16
For God so loved the world that He gave His only begotten Son, that whoever believes in Him should not perish but have everlasting life.

1 John 5:5
Who is he who overcomes the world, but he who believes that Jesus is the Son of God?

John 3:3
Jesus answered and said to him, "Most assuredly, I say to you, unless one is born again, he cannot see the kingdom of God."

Matthew 6:33
But seek first the kingdom of God and His righteousness, and all these things shall be added to you.

2 Corinthians 5:17
Therefore, if anyone is in Christ, he is a new creation; old things have passed away; behold, all things have become new.

Principles of Holy Spirit Baptism and Empowerment.

Every believer must be baptised in the Holy Ghost for effective living, divine regulation and regeneration and power generation through the Holy Spirt.

Matthew 3:11
I indeed baptize you with water unto repentance, but He who is coming after me is mightier than I, whose sandals I am not worthy to carry. He will baptize you with the Holy Spirit and fire.

Acts 1:8
But you shall receive power when the Holy Spirit has come upon you; and you shall be witnesses to Me in Jerusalem, and in all Judea and Samaria, and to the end of the earth.

Acts 2:4
And they were all filled with the Holy Spirit and began to speak with other tongues, as the Spirit gave them utterance.

Principle of Believer's Authority

Constantly exercising and using your authority as a believer without fail, without fear or contradictions keeps you above and victorious always. We have been authorised to use God's power. Satan is too cunning, too subtle and nicely goes about to beguile or deceive believers in order to steal, kill and destroy as he did to Adam and Eve in the garden of Eden. We are seated with Jesus Christ in heavenly places far above all principalities and powers and mights and dominions.

Luke 10:19
Behold, I give you the authority to trample on serpents and scorpions, and over all the power of the enemy, and nothing shall by any means hurt you.

Ephesians 1:20-21
Which He worked in Christ when He raised Him from the dead and seated Him at His right hand in the heavenly places, far above all principality and power and might and dominion, and every name that is named, not only in this age but also in that which is to come.

Ephesians 2:6
And raised us up together, and made us sit together in the heavenly places in Christ Jesus.

Principles of Prayer

Prayer is a two way communication or conversation between you and God. Prayer must be done effectively with combination of worship, praises, adoration, thanksgiving with the word of God and the power of the Holy Spirit. Praying with power in understanding and in tongues.

I Thessalonians 5:17
Pray without ceasing.

Philippians 4:6
Be anxious for nothing, but in everything by prayer and supplication, with thanksgiving, let your requests be made known to God.

Luke 18:1
Then He spoke a parable to them, that men always ought to pray and not lose heart.

Matthew 7:7
Ask, and it will be given to you; seek, and you will find; knock, and it will be opened to you.

Principle of Divine Healing

Jesus Christ brought the kingdom of heaven down to the earth, then the kingdom of God is within you if you've accepted Jesus as your Lord and Saviour. Healing and divine health are the nature of God and manifestations of this kingdom, such nature is not subject to sickness, disease and infirmities. God does not use sickness to teach His children a lesson, Jesus healed all our diseases. God wants you healthy, loaded with wellness and vitality fully fit for our assignment on earth.

Jesus Christ was anointed with the Holy Ghost and power, He went about doing good, healing all that were oppressed of the devil, for God was with Him. (ACTS 10:38)

PSALM 103:3
Who forgives all your iniquities, Who heals all your diseases.

1 PETER 2:24
Who Himself bore our sins in His own body on the tree, that we, having died to sins, might live for righteousness—by whose stripes you were healed.

3 JOHN 2
Beloved, I pray that you may prosper in all things and be in health, just as your soul prospers.

Principles of Faith

Whatever is not of faith is sin. God expects us to walk by faith not by sight and definitely not in fear. Faith is absolutely and total perpetual dependence and trust in the almighty God. We call those things that are not in physical existence into reality by instrumentation of faith. Mountains are moved by faith without doubting. Without faith it's impossible to please God, spiritual exercise requires faith, asking and receiving needs faith in action, the Christian life is a life of living by faith. Just like the body produces physical strength when nourished, the Spirit produces spiritual strength when nourished with God's word. That Spiritual strength is called faith.

MARK 11:22-24
So Jesus answered and said to them, "Have faith in God. For assuredly, I say to you, whoever says to this mountain, 'Be removed and be cast into the sea,' and does not doubt in his heart, but believes that those things he says will be done, he will have whatever he says. Therefore I say to you, whatever things you ask when you pray, believe that you receive them, and you will have them.

Hebrews 11:1, 6
Now faith is the substance of things hoped for, the evidence of things not seen…But without faith it is impossible to please Him, for he who comes to God must believe that He is, and that He is a rewarder of those who diligently seek Him.

Principle of Prosperity

Prosperity means to flourish, do well, blossom, have good successes and thrive, to have good fortune, affluence and accomplishments, to enjoy healthy relationships, wealth and wellness. It is God's will, covenant and plan that His people prosper and be in health even as their souls prosper. There's no glory in poverty, lack and degradation. True prosperity as a result of salvation, starts from the inside out. It's more than financial abundance or having loads of cash, if your spirit, soul and body is messed up and no peace, that's not prosperity but agony.

Proverbs 11:24-25
There is one who scatters, yet increases more; And there is one who withholds more than is right, But it leads to poverty. The generous soul will be made rich, And he who waters will also be watered himself.

Psalm 66:12
You have caused men to ride over our heads; We went through fire and through water; But You brought us out to rich fulfilment.

2 Corinthians 8:9
For you know the grace of our Lord Jesus Christ, that though He was rich, yet for your sakes He became poor, that you through His poverty might become rich.

2 Corinthians 9:8
And God is able to make all grace abound toward you, that you, always having all sufficiency in all things, may have an abundance for every good work.

3 John 1:2
Beloved, I pray that you may prosper in all things and be in health, just as your soul prospers.

Principle of Double Protection

There is an edge built around all the children of the Lord. An edge of fire, double protection, of thorns, angelic hosts, edges of the blood of Jesus Christ. You are protected from harm, plagues, afflictions, turbulence of life, visible and invisible forces, intimidations and harassments, wickedness, pestilence, evil and destructions, from assaults and molestations of darkness. Protected against all satanic summons and programmes that brings death, disaster, misfortunes, tragedies. Protected from discouragement, disappointments, despair, defeats, distress and disarray. The Lord guides and directs us through the paths and booby traps of life and minefields of the wicked.

COLOSSIANS 3:3
For you died, and your life is hidden with Christ in God.

ZECHARIAH 2:5
For I,' says the Lord, 'will be a wall of fire all around her, and I will be the glory in her midst.'

PSALM 125:2-3
As the mountains surround Jerusalem, So the Lord surrounds His people From this time forth and forever. For the scepter of wickedness shall not rest On the land allotted to the righteous, Lest the righteous reach out their hands to iniquity.

PSALM 91:1
He who dwells in the secret place of the Most High Shall abide under the shadow of the Almighty.

1 JOHN 5:4
For whatever is born of God overcomes the world. And this is the victory that has overcome the world—our faith.

2 PETER 1:4
By which have been given to us exceedingly great and precious promises, that through these you may be partakers of the divine nature, having escaped the corruption that is in the world through lust.

Chapter 4

THE BATTLE GATE

1 Timothy 6:12
Fight the good fight of faith, lay hold on eternal life, to which you were also called and have confessed the good confession in the presence of many witnesses.

Matthew 16:18-19
And I also say to you that you are Peter, and on this rock I will build My church, and the gates of Hades (hell) shall not prevail against it. And I will give you the keys of the kingdom of heaven, and whatever you bind on earth will be bound in heaven, and whatever you loose on earth will be loosed in heaven.

ENGAGE

{Combat, encounter, launch, strike, do battle with, fall on, give battle to, join battle with, take on etc}

Gate

An entry point, door, an opening, barrier, access point, passageway, entrance, point of departure, channel, pathway, a way in.

Psalm 24:7-10

Lift up your heads, O you gates! And be lifted up, you everlasting doors! And the King of glory shall come in. Who is this King of glory? The Lord strong and mighty, The Lord mighty in battle. Lift up your heads, O you gates! Lift up, you everlasting doors! And the King of glory shall come in. Who is this King of glory? The Lord of hosts, He is the King of glory. Selah

Isaiah 60:11

Therefore your gates shall be open continually; They shall not be shut day or night, That men may bring to you the wealth of the Gentiles, And their kings in procession.

Positive Gates

GATES OF PROGRESS

GATES OF PROSPERITY

GATES OF BREAKTHROUGH

GATES OF INFLUENCE

GATES OF FAVOUR, etc.

Negative Gates

GATE OF SORROW

GATE OF PAIN

GATE OF TROUBLE

GATE OF REGRET

GATE OF DEFEAT

GATE OF AFFLICTION, etc.

Gates - where city council meet to make decisions.

Decisions made over a territory.

Policy that influences territories.

THE BATTLE GATE

The devil knows it is more influential to put a territory into bondage by a simple law.

Luke 4:6-13 (territory of glory/wealth)
And the devil said to Him, "All this authority I will give You, and their glory; for this has been delivered to me, and I give it to whomever I wish. Therefore, if You will worship before me, all will be Yours." And Jesus answered and said to him, "Get behind Me, Satan! For it is written, 'You shall worship the Lord your God, and Him only you shall serve.'" Then he brought Him to Jerusalem, set Him on the pinnacle of the temple, and said to Him, "If You are the Son of God, throw Yourself down from here. For it is written: 'He shall give His angels charge over you, To keep you,' [11] and, 'In their hands they shall bear you up, Lest you dash your foot against a stone.'" And Jesus answered and said to him, "It has been said, 'You shall not tempt the Lord your God.'" Now when the devil had ended every temptation, he departed from Him until an opportune time.

Satan lays claim to earth's territory and its resources (rulers or delegated authority).

He has installed elders over nations, cities, boroughs, companies, governments, etc.

Ephesians 6:12
For we do not wrestle against flesh and blood, but against principalities, against powers, against the rulers of the darkness of this age, against spiritual hosts of wickedness in the heavenly places.

When a Christian enters a territory (such as getting a job), we assume things just work out. No, they don't. Job, position of influence, money, and marriage are spiritual entities to be contended for. Engage to take possession.

Romans 13:1
Let every soul be subject to the governing authorities. For there is no authority except from God, and the authorities that exist are appointed by God.

God is interested in authorities (territorial authorities); therefore, we must ask for the enlargement of coasts and territories and the ability to MANAGE.

Jesus knows our ministry will be of NO effect until we cast out devils and displace them for us to succeed.

Luke 10:19
Behold, I give you the authority to trample on serpents and scorpions, and over all the power of the enemy, and nothing shall by any means hurt you.

1 John 3:8
He who sins is of the devil, for the devil has sinned from the beginning. For this purpose the Son of God was manifested, that He might destroy the works of the devil.

Acts 10:38
How God anointed Jesus of Nazareth with the Holy Spirit and with power, who went about doing good and healing all who were oppressed by the devil, for God was with Him.

Jesus takes care of spiritual entities in a location He may be operating in, and that's why healing, deliverance, etc., take place. He never takes it for granted.

We must seize control of cities, nations, locations, and TERRITORIES in the name of Jesus.

Luke 10:17-19
Then the seventy returned with joy, saying, "Lord, even the demons are subject to us in Your name." And He said to them, "I saw Satan fall like lightning from heaven. Behold, I give you the authority to trample on serpents and scorpions, and over all the power of the enemy, and nothing shall by any means hurt you.

If God sends you to a nation OR city, YOU have an ALLOCATION in such a place, and you must take and use the authority and mandate of God in you that you carry to have A VOICE and INFLUENCE in the territory.

Money, Influence, and Perishing Souls

All these we must contend for, which means to engage and fight spiritually to take possession of THEM.

Luke 11:20 (cast out demons by the finger of God).
But if I cast out demons with the finger of God, surely the kingdom of God has come upon you.

Psalm 115:16 (gave us earth—heavens are the LORD'S).
The Heaven, even the heavens, are the Lord's; But the earth He has given to the children of men.

1 Corinthians 15:32 - (fought with beasts)
If, in the manner of men, I have fought with beasts at Ephesus, what advantage is it to me? If the dead do not rise, "Let us eat and drink, for tomorrow we die!"

Ephesians 6:12 – (wrestled with spirits)
For we do not wrestle against flesh and blood, but against principalities, against powers, against the rulers of the darkness of this age, against spiritual hosts of wickedness in the heavenly places.

Christian Business People

The competition are DEMONIC powers that want to bankrupt businesses and grind to a halt all business operations and frustrate entrepreneur spirits, dreams and visions

Acts 19:8
And he went into the synagogue and spoke boldly for three months, reasoning and persuading concerning the things of the kingdom of God.

Acts 17:17
Therefore he reasoned in the synagogue with the Jews and with the Gentile worshipers, and in the marketplace daily with those who happened to be there.

Prayer

EPHESIANS 2:5
Even when we were dead in trespasses, made us alive together with Christ (by grace you have been saved)...

EPHESIANS 1:19-21
And what is the exceeding greatness of His power toward us who believe, according to the working of His mighty power which He worked in Christ when He raised Him from the dead and seated Him at His right hand in the heavenly places, far above all principality and power and might and dominion, and every name that is named, not only in this age but also in that which is to come.

All GATES & TERRITORIES ARE Spiritual

Break and destroy all the power of Satan over such territories that are yours and chase out trespassers in the name of Jesus. Arrest all arresters of destiny. Contend with territorial spirits and guidance gods and lords and release territories from their grip and hold into God's bigger hands for prosperity and enduring good success.

REVELATION 12:11
And they overcame him by the blood of the Lamb and by the word of their testimony, and they did not love their lives to the death.

PHILIPPIANS 2:9-11
Therefore God also has highly exalted Him and given Him the name which is above every name, that at the name of Jesus every knee should bow, of those in heaven, and of those on earth, and of those under the earth, and that every tongue should confess that Jesus Christ is Lord, to the glory of God the Father.

TYPES OF TERRITORIES

Geographical

NATIONAL, INTERNATIONAL, CONTINENTAL, & INTERCONTINENTAL

Psalm 115:16
The heaven, even the heavens, are the Lord's; But the earth He has given to the children of men.

Psalm 24:1
The earth is the Lord's, and all its fullness, The world and those who dwell therein.

Political
GOVERNMENTAL, AUTHORITY, INFLUENCE, AND POWER

Romans 13:1
Let every soul be subject to the governing authorities. For there is no authority except from God, and the authorities that exist are appointed by God.

Ministerial
SPIRITUAL AUTHORITY, CHURCHES AND OTHER PARA MINISTRIES

Ephesians 1:22-23
And He put all things under His feet, and gave Him to be head over all things to the church, which is His body, the fullness of Him who fills all in all.

Acts 10:38
How God anointed Jesus of Nazareth with the Holy Spirit and with power, who went about doing good and healing all who were oppressed by the devil, for God was with Him.

Ephesians 4:11-12
And he gave some, apostles; and some, prophets; and some, evangelists; and some, pastors and teachers; For the perfecting of the saints, for the work of the ministry, for the edifying of the body of Christ.

Academics
CENTRE OF STUDY, LEARNING, CULTURE, INFORMATION, AND EXCELLENCE

Galatians 4:2
But is under tutors and governors until the time appointed of the father.

Family

INSTITUTION OF HOME RELATIONSHIP AND CENTREPIECE OF PARENTAGE AND ANCESTRY

Genesis 1:26-28
Then God said, "Let Us make man in Our image, according to Our likeness; let them have dominion over the fish of the sea, over the birds of the air, and over the cattle, over all the earth and over every creeping thing that creeps on the earth." So God created man in His own image; in the image of God He created him; male and female He created them. Then God blessed them, and God said to them, "Be fruitful and multiply; fill the earth and subdue it; have dominion over the fish of the sea, over the birds of the air, and over every living thing that moves on the earth."

Genesis 2:24-25
Therefore a man shall leave his father and mother and be joined to his wife, and they shall become one flesh. And they were both naked, the man and his wife, and were not ashamed.

Economics

COMMERCE AND INDUSTRIES, NATIONAL PROSPERITY. BUSINESSPEOPLE AND MARKETPLACE

Zechariah 1:17
Again proclaim, saying, 'Thus says the Lord of hosts: "My cities shall again spread out through prosperity; The Lord will again comfort Zion, And will again choose Jerusalem."'

Entertainment

SPORTS, ARTS AND CULTURE, MEDIA, ETC.

I break the power over my PROSPERITY and order the angel of God to move it in my direction (possess my possessions). I command access to my place of influence, even over the economy of this nation. I have territories to inherit and pass on to my biological and spiritual sons and daughters.

OBADIAH 1:17
But on Mount Zion there shall be deliverance, and there shall be holiness; the house of Jacob shall possess their possessions.

ACTS 8
Philip entered the city, and an end came to occultic power.

ACTS 8:9-11

But there was a certain man, called Simon, which beforetime in the same city used sorcery, and bewitched the people of Samaria, giving out that himself was some great one: To whom they all gave heed, from the least to the greatest, saying, This man is the great power of God. And to him they had regard, because that of long time he had bewitched them with sorceries.

ACTS 8:12-13
But when they believed Philip preaching the things concerning the kingdom of God, and the name of Jesus Christ, they were baptised, both men and women. Then Simon himself believed also: and when he was baptised, he continued with Philip, and wondered, beholding the miracles and signs which were done.

Anytime a kingdom prince enters a territory, all those prospering by occult power lose out and fail or become distressed.

A kingdom prince establishes and redistributes ownership and releases wealth because your prosperity that was locked up in occult power must be released

PRAYER/INTERCESSION

Every demon they've used in government, we freeze their accounts and end their witchcraft and sorcery in Jesus' name. I terminate everything working by occult power.

Run and chase out devils contracted by evil covenants. Run them out of town and business. Stop their activities and operations in the name of Jesus Christ.

MARK 11:23-24

For assuredly, I say to you, whoever says to this mountain, 'Be removed and be cast into the sea,' and does not doubt in his heart, but believes that those things he says will be done, he will have whatever he says. Therefore I say to you, whatever things you ask when you pray, believe that you receive them, and you will have them.

Prophesy things that must begin to happen for you from now on.

Declare enlargement season:

- Of coast
- Territory
- Habitation: Houses, Companies
- Money for ministries and kingdom operations.

Chapter 5

HOW TO ENGAGE

2 Corinthians 10:3-5
For though we walk in the flesh, we do not war according to the flesh. For the weapons of our warfare are not carnal but mighty in God for pulling down strongholds, casting down arguments and every high thing that exalts itself against the knowledge of God, bringing every thought into captivity to the obedience of Christ,.

ENGAGE

To combat, encounter, launch, strike, do battle with, fall on, give battle to, join battle with, take on, fight back.

- Battle is the seed for taking territories

The spiritual world actually exists. Life is not a funfair or jamboree but a battlefield.

For us to know how to engage in warfare and be victorious, we need to understand how the devil attacks.

God has designed and expects us to engage with the enemy.

Reasons to Know How to Engage

So that we KNOW when we're under satanic attack.

Attacks on our minds, marriage, money, academics, business, ministry, family, etc.

The way of attack is subtle, funny, crafty, concealed, silent, and not dramatic.

An example is answering questions from deceptive thoughts.

Genesis 3:1
Now the serpent was more cunning than any beast of the field which the Lord God had made. And he said to the woman, "Has God indeed said, 'You shall not eat of every tree of the garden?'"

For us to ACQUIRE valuable, good, important knowledge regarding life, family, finances, etc.

Proverbs 19:2
Also it is not good for a soul to be without knowledge, And he sins who hastens with his feet.

You can be able to HELP and teach others.

2 Timothy 2:2
And the things that you have heard from me among many witnesses, commit these to faithful men who will be able to teach others also.

To REDUCE Satan's chances and not outsmart us.

2 Corinthians 2:11
Lest Satan should take advantage of us; for we are not ignorant of his devices.

To be PREPARED specifically, as Satan is a thief and comes anytime and every time persistently.

Mark 13:33, 37
Take heed, watch and pray; for you do not know when the time is...And what I say to you, I say to all: Watch!

To know how to RESIST Satan's attack, using his same weapon to assault him back.

JAMES 4:7
Therefore submit to God. Resist the devil and he will flee from you.

To PROTECT ourselves from attacks and destruction.

EPHESIANS 6:11
Put on the whole armour of God, that you may be able to stand against the wiles of the devil.

To BREAK negative patterns & render ineffective satanic repeated attacks.

MATTHEW 4 - JESUS.
{OVERCAME ALL THE ATTACKS}

GENESIS 3 - ADAM & EVE
{ATTACKED WITH THE PATTERN OF 1 JOHN 2:15-17 AND LOST THE BATTLE}

Destroy all intentions of Satan because his attacks have no other thing than to kill, steal, and destroy.

JOHN 10:10
The thief does not come except to steal, and to kill, and to destroy. I have come that they may have life, and that they may have it more abundantly.

When the enemy attacks

{11 Symptoms of an attack}

1. Lack of spiritual passion.

The enemy comes to steal your tenacity for the things of God. Suddenly your prayer life seems stalled. Your commitment is tested and you can't seem to push though. You feel as though you are just going through the motions.

Numbers 13:31,33
But the men who had gone up with him said, "We are not able to go up against the people, for they are stronger than we." There we saw the giants (the descendants of Anak came from the giants); and we were like grasshoppers in our own sight, and so we were in their sight."

Romans 12:11
Not lagging in diligence, fervent in spirit, serving the Lord.

2. Extreme frustration.

During a spiritual attack the enemy uses a variety of circumstances to oppress the mind and bring great frustration. A person who is under siege finds themselves on edge and anxious.

Joshua 7:5
And the men of Ai struck down about thirty-six men, for they chased them from before the gate as far as Shebarim, and struck them down on the descent; therefore the hearts of the people melted and became like water.

3. Confusion About Purpose

During a spiritual attack there is often great confusion about spiritual direction. This is one of the chief goals of an attack, to get a believer out of destiny. That wrong move begins by bringing confusion.

Isaiah 30:21
Your ears shall hear a word behind you, saying, "This is the way, walk in it," Whenever you turn to the right hand Or whenever you turn to the left.

4. Lack of peace.

The enemy bombards the mind with various thoughts and ongoing temptation in order to rob peace. The mind becomes irritated and exhausted. The enemy does all that he can to bring mental fatigue.

1 Corinthians 14:33
For God is not the author of confusion but of peace, as in all the churches of the saints.

2 Chronicles 15:5
And in those times there was no peace to the one who went out, nor to the one who came in, but great turmoil was on all the inhabitants of the lands.

5. Unusually sluggish and tired.

A lack of energy and vitality are often the result of an extended attack. Certainly these issues can occur with natural problems, lack of sleep or health battles. In this case though, the root cause is the effect of prolonged spiritual battles.

Matthew 25:5
But while the bridegroom was delayed, they all slumbered and slept.

6. Strong urge to quit assignment.

Every believer is born with unique purpose. As God created a purpose for each believer, He also gave unique gifts and grace to fulfil that plan. When a person is living in the high calling, they will prosper in various areas: They will receive financial blessing by excelling in the area that God has called them to. They will feel satisfied and fulfilled living out their destiny.

Simply put, the enemy hates when a believer is boldly walking out their purpose and plan. He does all that he can to MOVE the Christian away from their destiny. During an attack he will overwhelm them with thoughts and desires to give up and abandon their post! This is one of his greatest purposes behind spiritual attacks.

John 21:3, 7
Simon Peter said to them, "I am going fishing." They said to him, "We are going with you also." They went out and immediately got into the boat, and that night they caught nothing. ...Therefore that disciple whom Jesus loved said to Peter, "It is the Lord!" Now when Simon Peter heard that it was the Lord, he put on his outer garment (for he had removed it), and plunged into the sea.

Luke 9.62
But Jesus said to him, "No one, having put his hand to the plow, and looking back, is fit for the kingdom of God."

7. Drawn back towards old bondages.

In a long spiritual battle a person is often pulled back towards negative cycles that they broke free from. The enemy wants to enslave them once again in the same old bondages. If he can discourage them bad enough to give into sin that they were free from then he can loose shame and condemnation upon them causing them to spiral down into deeper defeat.

Hebrews 10:26, 38-39
For if we sin willfully after we have received the knowledge of the truth, there no longer remains a sacrifice for sins, Now the just shall live by faith; But if anyone draws back, My soul has no pleasure in him." But we are not of those who draw back to perdition, but of those who believe to the saving of the soul.

8. Questioning direction and call that was one so clear.

As the enemy attacks the life of a believer he begins to give them reasons to give up on the very thing that God called them to. This is one of his master tools. He releases confusion, shame, intimidation and a variety of vile schemes to create a cloud of uncertainty. Again, his ultimate goal is to get a believer off the pathway of destiny, A person who is under attack may find themselves deeply questioning the road that they are travelling. Usually, they begin to reexamine decisions that were once crystal clear. Oftentimes a person in the midst of an attack will question prophetic words, spiritual breakthroughs and significant experiences that they had. This is a step towards moving backwards in the Spirit.

Numbers 22:12, 19, 21, 34
And God said to Balaam, "You shall not go with them; you shall not curse the people, for they are blessed." ...Now therefore, please, you also stay here tonight, that I may know what more the Lord will say to me." ...So Balaam rose in the morning, saddled his donkey, and went with the princes of Moab. ...And Balaam said to the Angel of the Lord, "I have sinned, for I did not know You stood in the way against me. Now therefore, if it displeases You, I will turn back."

9. Prayerlessness.

The attack of the enemy put a strain on our desire to pray, unwillingness and lack of courage to stand in Prayer cause our heart to be divided into several ways. We are pressed on every side, busy life, waste of time, spending too much time on social media and TV bring stress.

LUKE 18:1
Then He spoke a parable to them, that men always ought to pray and not lose heart.

LUKE 11:1
Now it came to pass, as He was praying in a certain place, when He ceased, that one of His disciples said to Him, "Lord, teach us to pray, as John also taught his disciples."

1 THESSALONIANS 5:17
Pray without ceasing.

10. Complaining and blame game.

When our heart is cluttered and become blind to favours and help of God all around us, we become too preoccupied with ways of life and couldn't see our way through. Unbelief and doubts fuels complaining. We blame families, church, establishment for our poor and unbearable situations around us.

GENESIS 3:12
Then the man said, "The woman whom You gave to be with me, she gave me of the tree, and I ate."

PHILIPPIANS 2:4
Let each of you look out not only for his own interests, but also for the interests of others.

JAMES 5:9
Do not grumble against one another, brethren, lest you be condemned. Behold, the Judge is standing at the door!

11. Wrong thoughts, shortcuts & evil imagination.

When we become full of hatred, jealousy and satanic emotions. It's a wrong cross over for enemy to put evil desires and thoughts in us

2 Corinthians 10:4-5
For the weapons of our warfare are not carnal but mighty in God for pulling down strongholds, casting down arguments and every high thing that exalts itself against the knowledge of God, bringing every thought into captivity to the obedience of Christ.

How to Engage

THE FIGHT BACK

1. When things are SUGGESTED to your mind, emotion, and body, especially when you're weak, tired, alone, or lonely with an intention to overcome, overwhelm, oppress, suppress, reduce, and destroy.

The Fight Back – The use & confession of God's word, saying or declaring that 'it is written'.

2 Corinthians 10:5
Casting down arguments and every high thing that exalts itself against the knowledge of God, bringing every thought into captivity to the obedience of Christ.

Luke 4:4
But Jesus answered him, saying, "It is written, 'Man shall not live by bread alone, but by every word of God.'"

Romans 10:10
For with the heart one believes unto righteousness, and with the mouth confession is made unto salvation.

2. Satan's attack is spiritual and uses DEMONS to fight you, including wicked spirits in heavenly places to prey on your flesh.

The Fight Back – You must not be battling, wrestling, or engaging in the flesh or being physical. It is a spiritual battle!

Ephesians 6:12
For we do not wrestle against flesh and blood, but against principalities, against powers, against the rulers of the darkness of this age, against spiritual hosts of wickedness in the heavenly places.

2 Corinthians 10:3-4
For though we walk in the flesh, we do not war according to the flesh. For the weapons of our warfare are not carnal but mighty in God for pulling down strongholds.

3. Because Satan attacks our loved ones and things that are most important and valuable to us in order to HURT us most, such as our children, spouses, marriage, source of income, ministry, integrity, health and reputation.

The Fight Back – Prayer - reliance on God. For God to build a wall of fire and protection around you and all that concerns you.

Zechariah 2:5
For I, 'says the Lord, 'will be a wall of fire all around her, and I will be the glory in her midst.'

Psalm 125:1-2
Those who trust in the Lord Are like Mount Zion, Which cannot be moved, but abides forever. As the mountains surround Jerusalem, So the Lord surrounds His people From this time forth and forever.

Colossians 3:3
For you died, and your life is hidden with Christ in God.

4. Due to his understanding of HUMAN NATURE, we are attacked.

Nature of Man
- Eye gate
- Lustfulness

Nature of Women
- Warfare
- Sweet and enticing words

Psalm 8:4
What is man that You are mindful of him, and the son of man that You visit him?

The Fight Back – Flee all appearances of evil. Maintain righteousness and holy living or lifestyle of godliness.

Galatians 5:16
I say then: Walk in the Spirit, and you shall not fulfill the lust of the flesh.

1 Thessalonians 5:22
Abstain from every form of evil.

5. Due to his UNDERSTANDING OF GOD, he will deceive you to do things to break fellowship with God. And when God is grieved, He leaves, and you're alone, giving room for Satan to operate mercilessly.

The Fight Back – Do not grieve the Holy Spirit of God.

Ephesians 4:30
And do not grieve the Holy Spirit of God, by whom you were sealed for the day of redemption.

6. Because of the INFORMATION Satan has gathered on you and his lies, he torments you and me and brings us into discouragement.

The Fight Back – Walk and keep dwelling in Love.

I John 4:18
There is no fear in love; but perfect love casts out fear, because fear involves torment. But he who fears has not been made perfect in love.

2 Timothy 1:7
For God has not given us a spirit of fear, but of power and of love and of a sound mind.

Joshua 1:9
Have I not commanded you? Be strong and of good courage; do not be afraid, nor be dismayed, for the Lord your God is with you wherever you go.

Chapter 6

WHEN TO ENGAGE

1 Timothy 6:12
Fight the good fight of faith, lay hold on eternal life, to which you were also called and have confessed the good confession in the presence of many witnesses.

Ecclesiastes 3:1, 8
To everything there is a season, A time for every purpose under heaven...A time to love, And a time to hate; A time of war, And a time of peace.

ENGAGE

- Combat, encounter, launch, strike, do battle with, fall on, give battle to, join battle with, take on, fight back.

- Battle is the seed for taking territories.

The spiritual world actually exists. Life is not a funfair or jamboree but a battlefield.

God has designed and expects us to engage with the enemy.

It's not just enough to be saved; you must know who God is and His ways of operation. You must know about the devil and his operations, so he won't take advantage of you and me. Therefore, we must not be ignorant about his devices.

For example, in **Matthew 16:23**, Jesus rebuked the devilish activity in Peter's life when he offered contrary counsel to Jesus Christ.

But He turned and said to Peter, "Get behind Me, Satan! You are an offense to Me, for you are not mindful of the things of God, but the things of men."

Luke 10:19
Behold, I give you the authority to trample on serpents and scorpions, and over all the power of the enemy, and nothing shall by any means hurt you.

Acts 26:18
To open their eyes, in order to turn them from darkness to light, and from the power of Satan to God, that they may receive forgiveness of sins and an inheritance among those who are sanctified by faith in Me.

Kinds of Devil's Power

1. Power to TEMPT.
{Entice, Seduce, Lead astray}.

James 1:13, 14
Let no one say when he is tempted, "I am tempted by God"; for God cannot be tempted by evil, nor does He Himself tempt anyone. But each one is tempted when he is drawn away by his own desires and enticed.

2. Power of FALSE DOCTRINE.

The fact that people are generally religious and seek to worship something, the devil tells them not to worship Jesus Christ.

1 Timothy 4:1-2
Now the Spirit expressly says that in latter times some will depart from the faith, giving heed to deceiving spirits and doctrines of demons...speaking lies in hypocrisy, having their own conscience seared with a hot iron...

3. Power to ACCUSE believers before God.

{Bring report against, make allegations against, incriminate and indict, find fault with, bring a charge against, false accusations}

1 Peter 5:8, 9
Be sober, be vigilant; because your adversary the devil walks about like a roaring lion, seeking whom he may devour. Resist him, steadfast in the faith, knowing that the same sufferings are experienced by your brotherhood in the world.

Zechariah 3:1
Then he showed me Joshua the high priest standing before the Angel of the Lord, and Satan standing at his right hand to oppose him.

Revelation 12:10
Then I heard a loud voice saying in heaven, "Now salvation, and strength, and the kingdom of our God, and the power of His Christ have come, for the accuser of our brethren, who accused them before our God day and night, has been cast down.

4. Power to DECEIVE.

{Mislead, Entrap, Falsely persuade, Ensnare, Trick, all forms of deceptions, lies and to defraud} by way of appearance, taste, touch, or influence.}

Revelation 20:3
And he cast him into the bottomless pit, and shut him up, and set a seal on him, so that he should deceive the nations no more till the thousand years were finished. But after these things he must be released for a little while.

5. Power of FALSE PROPHETS.

To teach all manner of adulterated doctrines so people won't know the truth. Erroneous statements, half truths, teachings to mislead, misinform, misinterpret Gods and His words, to divert people's attention from the truth and total salvation. Prophecy of lies and falsehoods and deception.

2 Peter 2:1-2
But there were also false prophets among the people, even as there will be false teachers among you, who will secretly bring in destructive heresies, even denying the Lord who bought them, and bring on themselves swift destruction. And many will follow their destructive ways, because of whom the way of truth will be blasphemed.

6. Power to OBSTRUCT.

{To hinder, Slow down, Weigh down, Cause delay}

1 Thessalonians 2:18
Therefore we wanted to come to you—even I, Paul, time and again—but Satan hindered us.

7. Power to BLIND & DEAF.

Blindfold people's minds with lies, care, worries, fear, darkness, deceitfulness of riches, etc., so they won't see, hear, or know the truth.

2 Corinthians 4:3-4
But even if our gospel is veiled, it is veiled to those who are perishing, whose minds the god of this age has blinded, who do not believe, lest the light of the gospel of the glory of Christ, who is the image of God, should shine on them.

Isaiah 6:9
And He said, "Go, and tell this people: 'Keep on hearing, but do not understand; Keep on seeing, but do not perceive.'

When Must We Engage

Isaiah 59:19
So shall they fear The name of the Lord from the west, And His glory from the rising of the sun; When the enemy comes in like a flood, The Spirit of the Lord will lift up a standard against him.

1. When our thinking about God, people, and ourselves is changing negatively because of what we're going through in life.

REMEMBER

Hebrews 13:5
Let your conduct be without covetousness; be content with such things as you have. For He Himself has said, "I will never leave you nor forsake you."

2. When our words and ways of saying them are getting contradictory because of pressures crushing us.

REMEMBER

Romans 10:10
For with the heart one believes unto righteousness, and with the mouth confession is made unto salvation.

Numbers 14:28
Say to them, 'As I live,' says the Lord, 'just as you have spoken in My hearing, so I will do to you.'

Psalm 107:2
Let the redeemed of Lord say so.

2 Corinthians 4:18
While we do not look at the things which are seen, but at the things which are not seen. For the things which are seen are temporary, but the things which are not seen are eternal.

Joshua 1:8
This Book of the Law shall not depart from your mouth, but you shall meditate in it day and night, that you may observe to do according to all that is written in it. For then you will make your way prosperous, and then you will have good success.

Job 6:25
How forceful are right words! But what does your arguing prove?

3. When fear is gripping our hearts. It is Satan's intention to keep you afraid of everything. He harasses and intimidates with fear. Fear has torment, but perfect love casts out fear.

REMEMBER

Be full of faith.

2 Corinthians 5:7
For We walk by faith and not by sight.

Romans 10:17
So then faith comes by hearing, and hearing by the word of God.

2 Timothy 1:7
For God has not given us a spirit of fear, but of power and of love and of a sound mind.

4. When our behaviour is changing and becoming carnal in the flesh. It leads to resentment, jealousy, envy, bitterness, and getting quarrelsome. Actions speaks louder than words

REMEMBER

Take mind of Christ.

Philippians 2:5
Let this mind be in you which was also in Christ Jesus…

Isaiah 55:8
"For My thoughts are not your thoughts, Nor are your ways My ways," says the Lord. "For as the heavens are higher than the earth, So are My ways higher than your ways, And My thoughts than your thoughts.

5. When we are being weighed down through oppression, suppression, regression, being worn out, discouraged, and depressed. Resist any negative low-level thinking and feelings of depression.

REMEMBER

Learn to rejoice at all times.

Philippians 4:4
Rejoice in the Lord always. Again I will say, rejoice!

Psalm 42:5, 11
Why are you cast down, O my soul? And why are you disquieted within me? Hope in God, for I shall yet praise Him For the help of His countenance.

6. When other voices are coming to us challenging:

– Our obedience and devotion to Christ

– Our yield to the Holy Spirit,

– Our submission to God,

– Our giving and love walk { general generosity}

It's of the devil and not of God almighty.

Three types of voices:

- GOD,
- YOU &
- Satan

REMEMBER

John 10:27
My sheep hear My voice, and I know them, and they follow Me.

7. When we are distracted, get our attention diverted, lose focus, and have our eyes kept off the path of destiny.

REMEMBER

Be filled with vision and revisit dreams and visions now and then.

Matthew 6:22
The lamp of the body is the eye. If therefore your eye is good, your whole body will be full of light.

Psalm 13:3
Consider and hear me, O Lord my God: lighten mine eyes, lest I sleep the sleep of death.

Psalm 119:18
Open my eyes, that I may see Wondrous things from Your law.

Chapter 7

GUARANTEED VICTORY

To be Guaranteed means:

{Assured, Secured, Done deal, Approved, Confirmed, Certain}

I John 5:4-5
For whatever is born of God overcomes the world. And this is the victory that has overcome the world—our faith. Who is he who overcomes the world, but he who believes that Jesus is the Son of God?

Victory means:

To Overcome, Breakthrough, Win, Triumph in an Engagement, Conquer, Achieve success, Defeat an opponent, Accomplish a mission.

Luke 10:17
Then the seventy returned with joy, saying, "Lord, even the demons are subject to us in Your name."

Colossians 2:15
Having disarmed principalities and powers, He made a public spectacle of them, triumphing over them in it.

Romans 8:37
Yet in all these things we are more than conquerors through Him who loved us.

GUARANTEES OF VICTORY

1. Victory is guaranteed and fixed even before battle started.

ROMANS 16:20
And the God of peace will crush Satan under your feet shortly. The grace of our Lord Jesus Christ be with you. Amen.

2. Victory is guaranteed because God loves us.

ROMANS 8:37
Yet in all these things we are more than conquerors through Him who loved us.

3. Victory is guaranteed because it's our comprehensive insurance policy. We're therefore covered.

LUKE 10:19
Behold, I give you the authority to trample on serpents and scorpions, and over all the power of the enemy, and nothing shall by any means hurt you.

4. Victory is guaranteed because we're anointed.

God's anointing on us removes burdens and destroys yokes.

PSALM 105:14-15
He permitted no one to do them wrong; Yes, He rebuked kings for their sakes, Saying, "Do not touch My anointed ones, And do My prophets no harm."

5. Victory is guaranteed because we are overcomers by faith through Christ Jesus, our Lord and Saviour.

JOHN 16:33
These things I have spoken to you, that in Me you may have peace. In the world you will have tribulation; but be of good cheer, I have overcome the world.

6. Victory is guaranteed because Christ dwells in us.

1 JOHN 4:4
You are of God, little children, and have overcome them, because He who is in you is greater than he who is in the world.

7. Victory is guaranteed because Jesus Christ won it and handed it over to us in righteousness.

Hebrews 1:8-9
But to the Son He says: "Your throne, O God, is forever and ever; A scepter of righteousness is the scepter of Your kingdom. You have loved righteousness and hated lawlessness; Therefore God, Your God, has anointed You With the oil of gladness more than Your companions.

2 Corinthians 5:21
For He made Him who knew no sin to be sin for us, that we might become the righteousness of God in Him.

Keys to enjoying Victory

Proverbs 4:20-27

Walk wisely

You have a part to play in responding to God's call, staying on His path, living wisely, and thereby making something beautiful out of your life. In this passage, we see four areas that you need to watch if you want to enjoy victory over temptation:

What you think about

You can choose what you think about. The life you lead will flow from your heart.

'Above all else, guard your heart, for it is the wellspring of life' (Proverbs 4:23).

You are to fill your heart with good things—especially the words of God (Proverbs 4:20–21).

They bring 'life' and 'health' (Proverbs 4:22).

Think about 'things that are true, noble, right, pure, lovely, admirable, excellent or praiseworthy' (Philippians 4:8).

What you say

ROMANS 10:10

For with the heart one believes unto righteousness, and with the mouth confession is made unto salvation.

Your words are powerful. Use them carefully.

'Put away perversity from your mouth; keep corrupt talk far from your lips' (**PROVERBS 4:24**).

It is said that the words of the tongue should have three gatekeepers:

Is it true?

Is it kind?

Is it necessary?

What you look at

2 CORINTHIANS 4:18

While we do not look at the things which are seen, but at the things which are not seen. For the things which are seen are temporary, but the things which are not seen are eternal.

Guard your eyes. Be careful what you look at (especially in this age of TV and the internet).

Let your eyes look straight ahead, fix your gaze directly before you'. Jesus warned that if you look at the wrong things, your *'whole body will be full of darkness'*. But he also said, *'If your eyes are good, your whole body will be full of light'*.

MATTHEW 6:22-23

The lamp of the body is the eye. If therefore your eye is good, your whole body will be full of light. But if your eye is bad, your whole body will be full of darkness. If therefore the light that is in you is darkness, how great is that darkness!

Where you go

You will avoid a lot of temptation if you are careful about where you go. 'Make level paths for your feet...keep your foot from evil' (**Proverbs 4:26–27**).

'Run with perseverance the race marked out' for you with your eyes fixed 'on Jesus... "Make level paths for your feet"'

Hebrews 12:1–2,12.
Therefore we also, since we are surrounded by so great a cloud of witnesses, let us lay aside every weight, and the sin which so easily ensnares us, and let us run with endurance the race that is set before us, looking unto Jesus, the author and finisher of our faith, who for the joy that was set before Him endured the cross, despising the shame, and has sat down at the right hand of the throne of God... Therefore strengthen the hands which hang down, and the feeble knees.

The Battle-Tools

THE WISDOM OF GOD

Wisdom is the application of knowledge acquired or gained by learning or training in what is true and right.

It is also insight, foresight, and intelligence about something. The use of experience to act and make sensible, strategic decisions.

Wisdom is, therefore, required in the life of a soldier of Christ, both for living and for spiritual warfare.

Wisdom makes us prudent, full of discretion, have fear of God, be of wise counsel and full of power.

Proverbs 4:7
Wisdom is the principal thing; Therefore get wisdom. And in all your getting, get understanding.

Proverbs 2:6
For the Lord gives wisdom; From His mouth come knowledge and understanding.

Proverbs 3:5
Trust in the Lord with all your heart, And lean not on your own understanding.

Ephesians 5:15-16
See then that you walk circumspectly, not as fools but as wise, redeeming the time, because the days are evil.

Proverbs 21:30-31
There is no wisdom nor understanding Nor counsel against the LORD. The horse is prepared against the day of battle: But safety is of the LORD.

THE NAME OF JESUS

The name of Jesus is above all names, be it the name of a nation, royal family, ordinary family, corporation, disease, or force, whether present on earth, in heaven, or under the earth. The name of Jesus is the greatest and mightiest of all times.

Everything and anyone called is subject to that name because the name of Jesus is highly exalted and superior to all other names. All authority and power that Jesus Christ has is vested in that name, and all believers have that power vested in them, which is the power of attorney to use that name at all times. Satan, all his demons and powers of darkness, tremble and go into bondage and defeat in the name of Jesus. Sickness, infirmities, ailments, afflictions, and diseases are destroyed in the name of Jesus.

The absolute measurement of the ability of Jesus Christ is the measure of the value of the name of Jesus. The name of Jesus is a great resource for ministry. It's the name that sin, Satan, demons, and dark powers fear and tremble at. It's the name of the Lord that is a strong tower. The name of Jesus gives victory in every battle of life and ministry.

Philippians 2:9-11
Therefore God also has highly exalted Him and given Him the name which is above every name, that at the name of Jesus every knee should bow, of those in heaven, and of those on earth, and of those under the earth, and that every tongue should confess that Jesus Christ is Lord, to the glory of God the Father.

Proverbs 18:10
The name of the Lord is a strong tower; The righteous run to it and are safe.

THE WORD OF GOD

God's word is the wisdom and mind and power of God. A believer must be saturated with the word of God to gain ground, be rooted, grounded, empowered, reinforced, and filled with the weight of glory. The Lord Jesus Christ used the weaponry of the word when He battled against the devil in the wilderness in the season of temptation. He spoke in faith and with authority, exercising His superiority over Satan and all his forces. You shall know the truth, and the truth shall make you free.

The word is light; if the word is not treated as light, we may not receive guidance through the darkness of life because darkness is not good. The word helps us locate where the traps of the enemy are hidden.

Psalm 36:9
For with You is the fountain of life; In Your light we see light.

Psalm 119:105
Your word is a lamp to my feet And a light to my path... The entrance of Your words gives light; It gives understanding to the simple.

God gives so much preference and credibility to His word because He magnifies His word above His name.

Psalm 138:2
I will worship toward Your holy temple, And praise Your name For Your lovingkindness and Your truth; For You have magnified Your word above all Your name.

When a believer speaks the word into a situation, that's God Himself being spoken because the word is God.

John 1:1
In the beginning was the Word, and the Word was with God, and the Word was God.

The kingdom of God is not in mere words but in power.

1 Corinthians 4:20
For the kingdom of God is not in word but in power.

Therefore, where the word of the King is, there is power. Hallelujah!

Ecclesiastes 4:8
Where the word of a king is, there is power; And who may say to him, "What are you doing?"

God sends His word, and it heals and delivers from destructions.

Psalm 107:20
He sent His word and healed them, And delivered them from their destructions.

The word of God is the spiritual offensive weapon called the sword of the Spirit.

Ephesians 6:17
And take the helmet of salvation, and the sword of the Spirit, which is the word of God.

The word of God is full of potency because it's alive and active, powerful and sharper than any two-edged sword.

Hebrews 4:12
For the word of God is quick, and powerful, and sharper than any two edged sword, piercing even to the dividing asunder of soul and spirit, and of the joints and marrow, and is a discerner of the thoughts and intents of the heart.

THE BLOOD OF JESUS

The precious blood of Jesus spotlessly shed on the Cross of Calvary is the greatest resource for victory for the believer. The devils cannot stand the pleading of the blood of Jesus in whatever situation. The blood cleanses, purges, washes, transforms, protects, and speaks of mercy, justice, and favours from God. The precious blood of Jesus Christ speaks better things than the blood of Abel. With our testimony as believers, we overcome the devil and all forces of darkness by the blood of Jesus and the word of our testimony.

HEBREWS 12:24
To Jesus the Mediator of the new covenant, and to the blood of sprinkling that speaks better things than that of Abel.

1 PETER 1:18
Knowing that you were not redeemed with corruptible things, like silver or gold, from your aimless conduct received by tradition from your fathers, but with the precious blood of Christ, as of a lamb without blemish and without spot.

HEBREWS 9:14
For if the blood of bulls and goats and the ashes of a heifer, sprinkling the unclean, sanctifies for the purifying of the flesh, how much more shall the blood of Christ, who through the eternal Spirit offered Himself without spot to God, cleanse your conscience from dead works to serve the living God?

REVELATIONS 19:13
He was clothed with a robe dipped in blood, and His name is called The Word of God.

REVELATIONS 12:11
And they overcame him by the blood of the Lamb and by the word of their testimony, and they did not love their lives to the death.

ANGELIC FORCES

There is so much evil, violence, wickedness and terror pouring from the pits of hell! But God's holy angels are stronger still. The saints will be preserved, the Church will prevail, and the Grand Reunion will take place on schedule.

When Elisha's servant woke up one morning, he saw that the evil people had come. "Oh no, my Lord! What shall we do?" the servant asked. "Don't be afraid," the prophet answered. "Those who are with us are more than those who are with them." Then, God opened the servant's eyes, and he saw they were protected.

2 Kings:16-17
So he answered, "Do not fear, for those who are with us are more than those who are with them." And Elisha prayed, and said, "Lord, I pray, open his eyes that he may see." Then the Lord opened the eyes of the young man, and he saw. And behold, the mountain was full of horses and chariots of fire all around Elisha.

This protection they had were angelic presence! The angels that showed up on the battlefield that day are called 'THE MIGHTY FORCES'. They serve in God's heavenly army. God is the Commander-in-Chief.

Psalm 34:7
The angel of the Lord encamps all around those who fear Him, And delivers them.

Hebrews 1:7,14
And of the angels He says: "Who makes His angels spirits And His ministers a flame of fire." …Are they not all ministering spirits sent forth to minister for those who will inherit salvation?

THE HOLY SPIRIT POWER

The Holy Spirit came from heaven. He was sent to earth by God the Father at the request of Jesus the Son. He came to testify of and glorify Jesus and to help believers, enabling them to live righteously. The Holy Spirit gives discernment regarding evil and deception. The Spirit of truth uses the Word of God to enable believers to stand firm by discriminating between good and evil, truth and lies.

The Holy Spirit empowers believers, granting them the strength to live in a manner that is impossible with mere human ability.

Believers are commanded to be filled with the Holy Spirit. Being "filled" means to make full, supply abundantly, and impart richly. We are filled with the Holy Spirit when we let the Word of God dwell richly in our hearts.

COLOSSIANS 3:16
Let the word of Christ dwell in you richly in all wisdom, teaching and admonishing one another in psalms and hymns and spiritual songs, singing with grace in your hearts to the Lord.

MICAH 3:8
But truly I am full of power by the Spirit of the Lord, And of justice and might, To declare to Jacob his transgression And to Israel his sin.

JOHN 14:17
The Spirit of truth, whom the world cannot receive, because it neither sees Him nor knows Him; but you know Him, for He dwells with you and will be in you.

The Holy Spirit is the source of power for believers and the entire Body of Christ.

ACTS 1:8
But you shall receive power when the Holy Spirit has come upon you; and you shall be witnesses to Me in Jerusalem, and in all Judea and Samaria, and to the end of the earth.

All the works, operations, and activities of the devil are destroyed by the power of the Holy Ghost.

ACTS 10:38
How God anointed Jesus of Nazareth with the Holy Spirit and with power, who went about doing good and healing all who were oppressed by the devil, for God was with Him.

All burdens are removed, and yokes are broken and destroyed by the anointing of the Holy Spirit.

ISAIAH 10:27
It shall come to pass in that day That his burden will be taken away from your shoulder, And his yoke from your neck, And the yoke will be destroyed because of the anointing oil.

Every believer has their strength exalted and anointed with fresh oil day by day, all by the power of the Holy Spirit.

Psalm 92:10
But my horn You have exalted like a wild ox; I have been anointed with fresh oil.

POWER OF PRAYER

Prayer is the means for enforcing God's will on earth. The hand that strikes down Satan is the power of the believer. A prayerless believer is powerless. Prayer is spiritual warfare. It is a battle axe. Prayer is a perpetual force against all powers of darkness in all their ramifications. It's the weapon to confront the enemies and staff to walk with God, the key of faith to open doors of blessings. Prayer is the key of the morning and bolt of the night, weapon in hour of conflict, defence in perilous moments.

When we pray, it's acting with God in His battle against evil, launching an assault to break down every opposing wall and demolishing every fortress of hell. In prayer weakness turns to strength, ordeal turns to explosive joy, despair into extravagant celebration, failure turns to success, galant defeat turns to outrageous victory, barriers are broken, irreversible turned around and become reversible, it gives heaven earthly licence for God to interfere, influence and invade our world.

James 5:16
Confess your trespasses to one another, and pray for one another, that you may be healed. The effective, fervent prayer of a righteous man avails much.

Acts 16:25-26
But at midnight Paul and Silas were praying and singing hymns to God, and the prisoners were listening to them... Suddenly there was a great earthquake, so that the foundations of the prison were shaken; and immediately all the doors were opened and everyone's chains were loosed.

1 Samuel 7:10
Now as Samuel was offering up the burnt offering, the Philistines drew near to battle against Israel. But the Lord thundered with a loud thunder upon the Philistines that day, and so confused them that they were overcome before Israel.

Prayer can release angels, the ministering spirits from God, to go on assignment on our behalf, and prayer keeps them operational.

ACTS 12:5-7
Peter was therefore kept in prison, but constant prayer was offered to God for him by the church.

....And when Herod was about to bring him out, that night Peter was sleeping, bound with two chains between two soldiers; and the guards before the door were keeping the prison.

.. Now behold, an angel of the Lord stood by him, and a light shone in the prison; and he struck Peter on the side and raised him up, saying, "Arise quickly!" And his chains fell off his hands.

2 KINGS 19:25
Then the angel of the Lord went out, and killed in the camp of the Assyrians one hundred and eighty-five thousand; and when people arose early in the morning, there were the corpses—all dead.

When we pray, man gives God the legal right and permission to interfere in earth's affairs.

MATTHEW 16:19
And I will give you the keys of the kingdom of heaven, and whatever you bind on earth will be bound in heaven, and whatever you loose on earth will be loosed in heaven.

It is giving heaven the licence to invade and influence earth. Prayer is man exercising his legal authority on earth to invoke heaven's influence on the planet.

2 CHRONICLES 7:14
If My people who are called by My name will humble themselves, and pray and seek My face, and turn from their wicked ways, then I will hear from heaven, and will forgive their sin and heal their land.

POWER OF PROPHETIC PRAISE

PSALM 47:6-7
Sing praises to God, sing praises! Sing praises to our King, sing praises! For God is the King of all the earth; Sing praises with understanding.

Praise means to:

– Offer grateful homage to God.

– Expressing Commendation, Admiration

– Appreciation and Compliment

– Celebration of the presence, glory and power of God

What PRAISES do

1. Brings God's COVERING over us.

PSALM 91:1-3
He who dwells in the secret place of the Most High Shall abide under the shadow of the Almighty. I will say of the Lord, "He is my refuge and my fortress; My God, in Him I will trust." Surely He shall deliver you from the snare of the fowler And from the perilous pestilence.

2. Provokes DIVINE INTERVENTION, which guarantees our divine victory.

Jehoshaphat

2 CHRONICLES 20:22
Now when they began to sing and to praise, the Lord set ambushes against the people of Ammon, Moab, and Mount Seir, who had come against Judah; and they were defeated.

Paul & Silas

ACTS 16:25-26
But at midnight Paul and Silas were praying and singing hymns to God, and the prisoners were listening to them. Suddenly there was a great earthquake, so that the foundations of the prison were shaken; and immediately all the doors were opened and everyone's chains were loosed.

3. Provokes the PRESENCE of God

God's presence makes a supernatural difference in our lives. It makes us smile in the storms of life.

PSALM 16:11
YOU WILL SHOW ME THE PATH OF LIFE; IN YOUR PRESENCE IS FULLNESS OF JOY; AT YOUR RIGHT HAND ARE PLEASURES FOREVERMORE.

4. Provokes DIVINE ENLARGEMENT, increase, and multiplication.

PSALM 67:5-6
Let the peoples praise You, O God; Let all the peoples praise You. Then the earth shall yield her increase; God, our own God, shall bless us.

5. Provokes DIVINE ELEVATION, promotion, and lifting.

David praised God seven times daily. He kept sheep, and he was elevated to the palace.

HABAKKUK 3:18-19
Yet I will rejoice in the Lord, I will joy in the God of my salvation. The Lord God is my strength; He will make my feet like deer's feet, And He will make me walk on my high hills. To the Chief Musician. With my stringed instruments.

6. Provokes DIVINE REVELATION, the Lord open our eyes of understanding and give grace to see the invisible and hear the inaudible. Secret things that belong to God are revealed unto us and our children forever.

2 KINGS 3:15
But now bring me a musician. Then it happened, when the musician played, that the hand of the Lord came upon him.

7. Provokes DIVINE PRESERVATION of lives, blessings, families, fortune, etc.

PSALM 66:8-9
Oh, bless our God, you peoples! And make the voice of His praise to be heard, Who keeps our soul among the living, And does not allow our feet to be moved.

8. Divine RESTORATION

Jesus lifted up His hands and gave thanks and God restore Lazarus.

JOHN 11:41, 43
Then they took away the stone from the place where the dead man was lying. And Jesus lifted up His eyes and said, "Father, I thank You that You have heard Me…Now when He had said these things, He cried with a loud voice, "Lazarus, come forth!"

9. Supernatural BREAKTHROUGH, unlimited and all-sufficient abundance.

JOSHUA 6:20
So the people shouted when the priests blew the trumpets. And it happened when the people heard the sound of the trumpet, and the people shouted with a great shout, that the wall fell down flat. Then the people went up into the city, every man straight before him, and they took the city.

10. Divine SUBSTITUTION, good name, and household safety.

JOSHUA 6:25
And Joshua spared Rahab the harlot, her father's household, and all that she had. So she dwells in Israel to this day, because she hid the messengers whom Joshua sent to spy out Jericho.

MATTHEW 1:5
Salmon begot Boaz by Rahab, Boaz begot Obed by Ruth, Obed begot Jesse.

11. Divine UNUSUAL HARVEST

PSALM 145:10, 15
All Your works shall praise You, O Lord, And Your saints shall bless You. The eyes of all look expectantly to You, And You give them their food in due season.

Chapter 8

POSSESSING YOUR POSSESSION

OBADIAH 1:17
But upon mount Zion shall be deliverance, and there shall be holiness; and the house of Jacob shall possess their possessions.

JOEL 2:32
And it shall come to pass, that whosoever shall call on the name of the LORD shall be delivered: for in mount Zion and in Jerusalem shall be deliverance, as the LORD hath said, and in the remnant whom the LORD shall call.

To possess something MEANS:

- To take ownership
- Claim something that belongs to you
- To have something, be gifted with a thing
- Take control of anything
- Take over and take charge
- To obtain and to secure
- To get your hands on

- Become the owner
- Take custody
- Take occupancy
- Contend for
- Impound, take back, battle militantly for

MATTHEW 11:12
And from the days of John the Baptist until now the kingdom of heaven suffereth violence, and the violent take it by force.

To take Possession, therefore, MEANS:

- Take what rightfully belongs to you
- Obtain divinely orchestrated assets such as:
- Inheritances
- Salvation packages & resources
- Territories
- Being head not tail; above not beneath
- Ideas, Creativity
- Properties

JOHN 3:31
He that cometh from above is above all: he that is of the earth is earthly, and speaketh of the earth: he that cometh from heaven is above all.

There are plans and provisions of God for His children. Those plans are of peace and not of evil. Those plans are to prosper and not harm His children and give a glorious future.

2 PETER 1:3
According as his divine power hath given unto us all things that pertain unto life and godliness, through the knowledge of him that hath called us to glory and virtue.

Ephesians 1:3
Blessed be the God and Father of our Lord Jesus Christ, who hath blessed us with all spiritual blessings in heavenly places in Christ...

There are:

– Things God wants you and me to have

– Places He wants you to be and get to

– Lifestyles He wants us to live

– Things He wants us to do for Him

– Where He wants us to go

Psalm 75:6-7
For exaltation comes neither from the east Nor from the west nor from the south. But God is the Judge: He puts down one, And exalts another.

To POSSESS, we need to claim, declare, fight for, take it by force, decree, receive our inheritance and all that belongs to us and all that we are meant to be etc., especially because of adversaries.

2 Corinthians 10:3-5
For though we walk in the flesh, we do not war after the flesh: (for the weapons of our warfare are not carnal, but mighty through God to the pulling down of strong holds;) casting down imaginations, and every high thing that exalteth itself against the knowledge of God, and bringing into captivity every thought to the obedience of Christ.

Fighting the Adversaries

{Satan, mental blockage, negative thoughts, wrong imaginations}, etc.

We fight the adversary with:

1. Our PRAYERS.

Intercede and bring peace, promotion, provision, and protection. Root out, overthrow, pull down stronghold and build up and take over territories.

Philippians 4:6-7
Be anxious for nothing, but in everything by prayer and supplication, with thanksgiving, let your requests be made known to God; and the peace of God, which surpasses all understanding, will guard your hearts and minds through Christ Jesus.

2. Our PRINCIPLES

Speaking faith-filled words and setting long-term values to build on. Constant in season and out of season.

Romans 10:9-10, 17
That if you confess with your mouth the Lord Jesus and believe in your heart that God has raised Him from the dead, you will be saved. For with the heart one believes unto righteousness, and with the mouth confession is made unto salvation.

3. Our PROMISES

There is a need for reassurance of God's presence against all insecurities, both spiritual and physical.

Romans 8:31
What then shall we say to these things? If God is for us, who can be against us?

4. Our PERSISTENCE

Never quitting, never giving up, no retreat, no surrender, not absconding, especially when time is hard and things are tough or rough.

Galatians 6:9
And let us not grow weary while doing good, for in due season we shall reap if we do not lose heart.

5. Our PATIENCE

Taking postures of victory while we wait for testimonies, better reports, good news, victory reports, breakthroughs, and breaking forth.

James 1:2-4
My brethren, count it all joy when you fall into various trials, knowing that the testing of your faith produces patience. But let patience have its perfect work, that you may be perfect and complete, lacking nothing.

6. We take our STAND in contention and warfare. We maintain our posture, rooted and grounded.

Ephesians 6:13
Therefore take up the whole armour of God, that you may be able to withstand in the evil day, and having done all, to stand.

Principles of Possessing Your Possession

1. SATURATION OF REVELATIONS

Put more word of God in you so you can have the weight of glory on you.

Load yourself with more truth in you than any other trash, lies, contradictions, constant negative news, and wrong confessions.

Program your soul with God's word.

See, hear, and speak consistently the word of God.

Psalm 1:1-3
Blessed is the man Who walks not in the counsel of the ungodly, Nor stands in the path of sinners, Nor sits in the seat of the scornful...But his delight is in the law of the Lord, And in His law he meditates day and night...He shall be like a tree Planted by the rivers of water, That brings forth its fruit in its season, Whose leaf also shall not wither; And whatever he does shall prosper.

Joshua 1:8
This Book of the Law shall not depart from your mouth, but you shall meditate in it day and night, that you may observe to do according to all that is written in it. For then you will make your way prosperous, and then you will have good success.

John 17:17
Sanctify them by Your truth. Your word is truth.

Hebrews 4:12
For the word of God is living and powerful, and sharper than any two-edged sword, piercing even to the division of soul and spirit, and of joints and marrow, and is a discerner of the thoughts and intents of the heart.

Jeremiah 15:16
Your words were found, and I ate them, And Your word was to me the joy and rejoicing of my heart; For I am called by Your name, O Lord God of hosts.

2. SUPERNATURAL RELIANCE

Depend on God. Don't rely on yourself, other people, or certain systems of the world.

Trust in God only. There's enough power from God to change your situation. Rest on God beyond all reasonable doubts, without fear and contradictions.

Proverbs 3:5-7
Trust in the Lord with all your heart, And lean not on your own understanding…In all your ways acknowledge Him, And He shall direct your paths…Do not be wise in your own eyes; Fear the Lord and depart from evil.

John 15:5
I am the vine, you are the branches. He who abides in Me, and I in him, bears much fruit; for without Me you can do nothing.

Matthew 19:26
But Jesus looked at them and said to them, "With men this is impossible, but with God all things are possible."

3. SATANIC RESISTANCE

Stand against and reject all satanic, demonic, and devilish influences and oppositions in your life. Resist consistently. Refute all allegations and rebuff false claims and wrong suggestions.

JAMES 4:7
Therefore submit to God. Resist the devil and he will flee from you.

I PETER 5:8-10
Be sober, be vigilant; because your adversary the devil walks about like a roaring lion, seeking whom he may devour. ..Resist him, steadfast in the faith, knowing that the same sufferings are experienced by your brotherhood in the world. ..But may the God of all grace, who called us to His eternal glory by Christ Jesus, after you have suffered a while, perfect, establish, strengthen, and settle you.

4. SACRIFICIAL RESPONSES

Going over and above your initial expectations. Put more effort beyond normal and usual despite what we are seeing and experiencing.

PROVERBS 23:18
For surely there is an end; And thine expectation shall not be cut off.

This enables God to make a difference to help and bless us beyond our talents, gifts, and skills.

ROMANS 12:1
I beseech you therefore, brethren, by the mercies of God, that you present your bodies a living sacrifice, holy, acceptable to God, which is your reasonable service.

EPHESIANS 3:20
Now to Him who is able to do exceedingly abundantly above all that we ask or think, according to the power that works in us.

5. STEADFAST RESOLVE

Keep confessing what you want or desire without fail. You obtain the promise after doing God's will. Be determined and courageous. A closed mouth is a closed destiny.

I CORINTHIANS 15:58
Therefore, my beloved brethren, be steadfast, immovable, always abounding in the work of the Lord, knowing that your labor is not in vain in the Lord.

Isaiah 50:7
For the Lord God will help Me; Therefore I will not be disgraced; Therefore I have set My face like a flint, And I know that I will not be ashamed.

Hebrews 10:23, 35-36
Let us hold fast the profession of our faith without wavering; (for he is faithful that promised;) Cast not away therefore your confidence, which hath great recompense of reward. For ye have need of patience, that, after ye have done the will of God, ye might receive the promise.

6. SPIRITUAL REST

When you rest on God no matter what, you find your solace, confidence, and peace with Him. You're just at peace; nothing is missing or broken. No shaking!

Isaiah 26:3
You will keep him in perfect peace, Whose mind is stayed on You, Because he trusts in You.

Exodus 14:14
The Lord will fight for you, and you shall hold your peace.

Hebrews 4:1
Let us therefore fear, lest, a promise being left us of entering into his rest, any of you should seem to come short of it.

7. SOVEREIGN REWARDS

God becomes committed to show up no matter what. He is our rewarder.

Hebrews 11:6
But without faith it is impossible to please Him, for he who comes to God must believe that He is, and that He is a rewarder of those who diligently seek Him.

Genesis 15:1
After these things the word of the Lord came to Abram in a vision, saying, "Do not be afraid, Abram. I am your shield, your exceedingly great reward."

Chapter 9

OVERCOMING NEGATIVE THOUGHTS

2 Corinthians 10:3-5
For though we walk in the flesh, we do not war according to the flesh. For the weapons of our warfare are not carnal but mighty in God for pulling down strongholds, casting down arguments and every high thing that exalts itself against the knowledge of God, bringing every thought into captivity to the obedience of Christ.

Thoughts are:

1. Ideas you have in your mind
2. Capacity for reasoning
3. Imagination
4. Reflection, Consideration
5. Meditation, Recollection
6. Intentions, Design, Purpose
7. Expectations
8. Considerations
9. Opinions
10. Intellectual activity

Types of Negative Thoughts

1. Perverted thoughts of OFFENCES

(Deception, hurts, broken heart, wounds, bitterness)

MARK 11:25-26
And whenever you stand praying, if you have anything against anyone, forgive him, that your Father in heaven may also forgive you your trespasses. But if you do not forgive, neither will your Father in heaven forgive your trespasses.

LUKE 17:1
Then He said to the disciples, "It is impossible that no offences should come, but woe to him through whom they do come!"

PSALM 119:165
Great peace have those who love Your law, And nothing causes them to stumble.

2. Perverted thoughts of OVERWHELM

If I can do all things through Christ who strengthens me, I refuse to be overwhelmed, overcome, and intimidated to deal with my limitations.

1 CORINTHIANS 6:12
All things are lawful for me, but all things are not helpful. All things are lawful for me, but I will not be brought under the power of any.

GALATIANS 2:20
I have been crucified with Christ; it is no longer I who live, but Christ lives in me; and the life which I now live in the flesh I live by faith in the Son of God, who loved me and gave Himself for me.

3. Perverted thoughts of OPPORTUNITY

Thoughts to sin, do evil, and go contrary to the truth and righteousness.

(Thoughts to steal, assault, immorality, etc. Watch your thoughts)

1 CORINTHIANS 10:13
No temptation has overtaken you except such as is common to man; but God is faithful, who will not allow you to be tempted beyond what you are able,

but with the temptation will also make the way of escape, that you may be able to bear it.

Genesis 39:8
But he refused and said to his master's wife, "Look, my master does not know what is with me in the house, and he has committed all that he has to my hand. There is no one greater in this house than I, nor has he kept back anything from me but you, because you are his wife. How then can I do this great wickedness, and sin against God?"

4. Perverted thoughts of ORIENTATION

Sexual orientation.

Romans 1:21,24
Because, although they knew God, they did not glorify Him as God, nor were thankful, but became futile in their thoughts, and their foolish hearts were darkened... Therefore God also gave them up to uncleanness, in the lusts of their hearts, to dishonour their bodies among themselves.

5. Perverted thoughts of SOCIAL JUSTICE

As we lift Jesus high, it is inevitable that themes of compassion and social justice will begin to emerge in our lives. Feeding the poor, rescuing the orphans, or standing up for the victims of modern slavery is not just a charity issue—it is a worship issue. To act otherwise is a perversion.

Micah 6:8
He has shown you, O man, what is good; And what does the Lord require of you But to do justly, To love mercy, And to walk humbly with your God?

Lamentations 3:36
Or subvert a man in his cause—The Lord does not approve.

Sources of Thoughts

1. From the devil.

Demonic intrusion, invasion, programmed summons, ruthless aggression, aggravated, perverted ideas and suggestions.

Ephesians 6:16
Above all, taking the shield of faith with which you will be able to quench all the fiery darts of the wicked one.

2. Society-initiated thoughts.

Influence of culture and thinking of time, philosophy, and society changes.

Colossians 2:8
Beware lest anyone cheat you through philosophy and empty deceit, according to the tradition of men, according to the basic principles of the world, and not according to Christ.

3. Thoughts from myself.

Self-intimidated, initiated thoughts and suggestions based on my personal philosophy, opinions, people, and general personal belief systems.

Proverbs 23:7
For as he thinks in his heart, so is he. "Eat and drink!" he says to you, But his heart is not with you.

4. Spiritual-initiated thoughts from God.

God orders my thoughts if I'm sensitive to the Holy Spirit.

It demonstrates that my thoughts are from God. It lines up with His will, and I succeed in all endeavours.

Proverbs 16:3-4
Commit your works to the Lord, And your thoughts will be established. The Lord has made all for Himself, Yes, even the wicked for the day of doom.

5. Spiritual initiated thoughts from the Bible.

Divine revelation opens my eyes, changes me, and renews my mind. When I read the scriptures, it changes and transforms my thinking.

OVERCOMING NEGATIVE THOUGHTS

PHILIPPIANS 4:8
Finally, brethren, whatever things are true, whatever things are noble, whatever things are just, whatever things are pure, whatever things are lovely, whatever things are of good report, if there is any virtue and if there is anything praiseworthy—meditate on these things.

Dealing with Thoughts

Then there are those who, instead of looking through the windscreen of hope and possibility, have purposefully placed their lives in reverse and are moving backwards.

They've believed lies—words spoken that are simply not true, statements that have lowered their self-esteem or changed the focus of their hearts—so that they now feel as though they'll never move past this point in time.

They notice their peers and friends moving forward, but they fail to believe in God's ability to change the direction of their own lives.

Therefore, they become stuck in feelings of defeat and disillusionment. If any of these describe your life, I want to assure you that you're not alone.

You could, therefore, handle or deal with your thoughts using the following:

1. Transform your thinking and thought patterns, and you will be in control. Renew your mind, refresh and overhaul your mindset.

PROVERBS 16:3
Commit your works to the Lord, and your thoughts will be established.

2. You are the product of your thought life.

I am conformed to my thinking, whether good or bad.

The essence of who I am is generated by my thinking.

Matthew 12:35
A good man out of the good treasure of his heart brings forth good things, and an evil man out of the evil treasure brings forth evil things.

3. Acknowledge the destruction perverted thoughts can cause.

Isaiah 59:7
Their feet run to evil, And they make haste to shed innocent blood; Their thoughts are thoughts of iniquity; Wasting and destruction are in their paths.

4. Turn your whole life around by changing your thoughts.

Proverbs 12:5
The thoughts of the righteous are right, But the counsels of the wicked are deceitful.

Advance From Thought to Inspiration

My THOUGHTS Become

My INTELLECT (My Basis to process Information)

Which enables my

INSTINCT (The Impromptu responses I give to situation)

This fuels my

IMAGINATION (This is my ability to think resourcefully)

To become my

IMPRESSIONS (This affects my emotional state)

I am who I am and know I'm coming out of trials and tribulations better than before.

Acts 26:2
I think myself happy, King Agrippa, because today I shall answer for myself before you concerning all the things of which I am accused by the Jews.

My impressions become my

INSPIRATION (this is a creative motivation for setting things in order)

2 Timothy 3:16
All Scripture is given by inspiration of God, and is profitable for doctrine, for reproof, for correction, for instruction in righteousness...

Job 32:8
But there is a spirit in man, And the breath (inspiration) of the Almighty gives him understanding.

Measuring my Thoughts

My thoughts are measured against the righteousness of the word of God and not against philosophy, legalism, or any vague belief systems.

Hebrews 4:12
For the word of God is living and powerful, and sharper than any two-edged sword, piercing even to the division of soul and spirit, and of joints and marrow, and is a discerner of the thoughts and intents of the heart.

My thoughts become the pathway or roadblock to my success.

Jeremiah 29:11
For I know the thoughts that I think toward you, says the Lord, thoughts of peace and not of evil, to give you a future and a hope.

If untrue or contrary thoughts come, I reject, refuse, and choose not to entertain such thoughts.

Philippians 4:8
Finally, brethren, whatever things are true, whatever things are noble, whatever things are just, whatever things are pure, whatever things are lovely, whatever things are of good report, if there is any virtue and if there is anything praiseworthy—meditate on these things.

My thoughts must not feed on hearsay but on the truth, which is the word of God.

John 17:17
Sanctify them by Your truth. Your word is truth.

How to Measure

Through kingdom SATURATION.

Meditating on the word of God day and night.

Joshua 1:8
This Book of the Law shall not depart from your mouth, but you shall meditate in it day and night, that you may observe to do according to all that is written in it. For then you will make your way prosperous, and then you will have good success.

Through Kingdom or positive SPEAKING.

My life is filled with the fruits of my lips. Change your critical, judgemental spirit to a complementary one, from being pessimistic to being optimistic, from being negative to positive talker. Speak with grace and appreciate people.

Proverbs 18:21
Death and life are in the power of the tongue, And those who love it will eat its fruit.

3. Changing your SURROUNDINGS.

Our surroundings have a strong effect on our thinking.

The prodigal son changed his thinking and surroundings amongst pigs and came to himself.

Luke 15:17
But when he came to himself, he said, 'How many of my father's hired servants have bread enough and to spare, and I perish with hunger!'

Psalm 1:1-3
Blessed is the man Who walks not in the counsel of the ungodly, Nor stands in the path of sinners, Nor sits in the seat of the scornful; But his delight is in the law of the Lord, And in His law he meditates day and night. He shall be like a tree planted by the rivers of water, That brings forth its fruit in its season, Whose leaf also shall not wither; And whatever he does shall prosper.

Chapter 10

TAKING AUTHORITY

{Essential Authority}

Authority in your Mouth

PROVERBS 18:19-21
A brother offended is harder to win than a strong city, And contentions are like the bars of a castle. A man's stomach shall be satisfied from the fruit of his mouth; From the produce of his lips he shall be filled. Death and life are in the power of the tongue, And those who love it will eat its fruit.

Authority means:

- To have the legal power to make and enforce the law
- Power of determination in an outcome
- Vested power to influence, delegate, control
- Ability to make decisions

God's will for me is to live an overcomer's life. But we have an adversary that wants to steal, kill, and destroy.

JOHN 10:10
The thief does not come except to steal, and to kill, and to destroy. I have come that they may have life, and that they may have it more abundantly.

God put man in charge of the earth.

PSALM 115:16
The heaven, even the heavens, are the Lord's; But the earth He has given to the children of men.

We must take responsibility for our leadership on the earth.

JOHN 16:33
These things I have spoken to you, that in Me you may have peace. In the world you will have tribulation; but be of good cheer, I have overcome the world.

We must respond the right way to overcome what we are going through.

ROMANS 8:37
Yet in all these things we are more than conquerors through Him who loved us.

Put enough pressure upon your tongue to exercise authority (spoken word gives victory).

We can move heaven on earth. So, you can have what you say.

MARK 11:23-24
For assuredly, I say to you, whoever says to this mountain, 'Be removed and be cast into the sea,' and does not doubt in his heart, but believes that those things he says will be done, he will have whatever he says...Therefore I say to you, whatever things you ask when you pray, believe that you receive them, and you will have them.

Dealing with thoughts (dealing and responding the right way with our mouth). You don't fight thoughts with thoughts but by speaking out against wrong thoughts. Also, when there is an offence, and we do not respond in the right way, relationships can be destroyed through the power of mouth, e.g., marriage/business relationship/family relationship/long-lasting friendship.

Types of Spiritual Authority

a. **Creative Authority** (build new things, structure)

b. **Salvation Authority** (speak and win lost souls)

c. **Situation Authority** (speak to storm)

d. **Commission Authority** (ministry to cast out devil)

e. **Corporate Authority** (agreement/unity)

f. **Condition Authority** (when I obey God, my authority over the wicked is strong)

MATTHEW 8:5-10
Here, a centurion whose servant was sick came to Jesus and spoke the word at a spiritual level over a situation.

Declare the word and take authority.

EPHESIANS 6:12
For we do not wrestle against flesh and blood, but against principalities, against powers, against the rulers of the darkness of this age, against spiritual hosts of wickedness in the heavenly places.

The roots of most offences start with thoughts. Ephesians 6:16 (shield of faith to quench fiery darts of the devil fired at us).

2 CORINTHIANS 10:4-5
For though we walk in the flesh, we do not war according to the flesh: (For the weapons of our warfare are not carnal but mighty in God for pulling down strongholds), casting down arguments and every high thing that exalts itself against the knowledge of God, bringing every thought into captivity to the obedience of Christ...

Satanic thoughts are intrusive, but our interpretations are most important to get us out of offences into victory.

In order to fight to maintain good quality relationships in marriage, ministry, friendship, or business, we must police our thoughts to be victorious as we respond and cast down and cast out wicked suggestions.

MATTHEW 6:31
Take no thought "Saying".

Respond oppositely and against slanderous, wicked thoughts.

Don't let negative thoughts take root in you. Instead, respond to them with authority.

When you don't respond to negative thoughts, they stay in your

- Heart, and goes to your;
- Mouth and when you speak to;
- Others, it gains grounds and grips you, giving the devil a foothold

Be thankful and grateful for what you have; murmuring and complaining usually give grounds to Satan.

PROVERBS 4:23
Guard your hearts with diligence for out of it are the issues of life.

You must have concrete evidence to draw a conclusion on a matter, or your words may ensnare you.

6 things required for spiritual warfare using your mouth

Discernment

– Ability to know good and evil.

Declaration

– Speaking words over negative thoughts.

Demand

- Exercising my authority

Demeanour
– Speaking my way out of the pit.

Discipline
– Building boundaries as I speak words repeatedly till victory is assured.

Discovery
– Coming to the point and final conclusion that I'm redeemed and walking in victory over the devil, knowing he has no right to win over me.

Authority Over Shame

ROMANS 9:33
As it is written: "Behold, I lay in Zion a stumbling stone and rock of offence, And whoever believes on Him will not be put to shame."

Jesus Christ, with His precious blood, paid the price and died for our deliverance from the devastations of life, such as sickness, sin, suffering, and shame.

Shame Means

- Demoralising intensifying emotional pain caused by consciousness of guilt, dishonour, defeat, failure, shortcomings, disgrace, disrespect, disapproval, disappointment, and rejection.
- Painful traits and trauma that put us down, stigmatise, devalue, and make us have toxic thoughts of abuse, torture, arrest, pain, rape, divorce, failure, losses, bankruptcy, imprisonment, and a dysfunctional lifestyle.
- Dark clouds that hang over people and prevent freedom and confident living.
- Feelings of humiliation, intimidation, hopelessness, and worthlessness.
- Shame is a real pain that erects barriers and makes us:

1. Proud, bitter, and angry. Trust is lost, and we always lash out to cover up.

2. Alters our decisions because we are afraid to make decisions.

3. It affects us in our next relationship because we keep remembering what other people did against us in the past.

4. It affects our participation because we can't give 100% to new employers because of pain, mistreatment, and shame caused by previous employment.

5. Finding it hard to believe that God can use us in our destiny pursuits.

6. Alters our defences due to low self-esteem.

7. Defines, messes, and defiles our lives, including stealing our confidence and joy.

Some greatness is trapped within us and can't be released until we get rid of shame.

Types of Shame

1. Sovereign shame.

When shame is used as judgement against our enemies.

PSALM 35:26
Let them be ashamed and brought to mutual confusion Who rejoice at my hurt; Let them be clothed with shame and dishonour Who exalt themselves against me.

2. Social shame.

Product of violation of certain protocol in a place or area or public.

ACTS 19:14-16
Also there were seven sons of Sceva, a Jewish chief priest, who did so. And the evil spirit answered and said, "Jesus I know, and Paul I know; but who are you?" Then the man in whom the evil spirit was leaped on them, overpowered them, and prevailed against them, so that they fled out of that house naked and wounded.

3. Sin shame.

Product of misbehaviour and disobedient life leading to a sense of guilt and shame.

JOHN 8:34
Jesus answered them, "Most assuredly, I say to you, whoever commits sin is a slave of sin."

4. Satanic shame.

Demonic accusation is when the devil comes to accuse you with negative thoughts and define you by episodes of life and what has happened in the past.

REVELATION 12:10
Then I heard a loud voice saying in heaven, "Now salvation, and strength, and the kingdom of our God, and the power of His Christ have come, for the accuser of our brethren, who accused them before our God day and night, has been cast down."

5. Scrutinising shame.

Correction and rebuke after someone has done wrong things.

2 THESSALONIANS 3:14
And if anyone does not obey our word in this epistle, note that person and do not keep company with him, that he may be ashamed.

6. Demoralising shame.

When Satan uses our error to disqualify us from moving forward and succeeding. Also pumping us with thoughts to encroach us and to talk us into misbehaviour and talk us out of promises of God.

2 CORINTHIANS 2:11
Lest Satan should take advantage of us; for we are not ignorant of his devices.

Shame Attacks

ROMANS 8:1-2
There is therefore now no condemnation to those who are in Christ Jesus, who do not walk according to the flesh, but according to the Spirit. For the law of the Spirit of life in Christ Jesus has made me free from the law of sin and death.

I CORINTHIANS 10:13
No temptation has overtaken you except such as is common to man; but God is faithful, who will not allow you to be tempted beyond what you are able, but with the temptation will also make the way of escape, that you may be able to bear it.

1. Conception

Satan always wants you to own your shame through guilt obtained from the following:

- Misbehaviour
- Condemnation
- Shortcomings
- Unconscious dishonour
- Unconscious disrespect

2. Concentration

Satan wants you to concentrate on negative, bad, or disadvantageous events and think about them over and over, again and again.

- He wants you to feel pain
- He wants to steal your joy

3. Conversation

Satan wants you to talk about negative situations and occurrences over and over and all over again until you're stuck and sink so low, lower, and lower. Totally deflated.

4. Compilation

To pile up files and records of shame issues, archives of past and present issues.

5. Consideration

When you start making decisions based on shame issues.

Source of Shame Situations

1. Personal shame episodes...

Such as:

- Dropping out of school and letting others down.
- Being kicked out of the church or fellowship or delisted from a professional body due to misconduct.
- Probably jail time.
- Police arrest.
- Pregnant out of wedlock.

2. Predator malicious abuse

Such as:

- Violations like rape.
- Exposure of secrets to hurt one another.
- Divorce.

3. Positional association

When you pick up shame as a result of association with people others want to keep away from.

4. Persecution-shame scenario

Listening to undue criticism from people over some time repeatedly, which keeps you from genuine repentance.

Deliverance From Shame

My worth is not based on my:

- Accomplishments, qualifications, and know-how
- Performances
- Position
- Possession

My worth is based on the PRICE paid by the blood of Jesus Christ.

My value with God has not changed, no matter what evil has been done against me.

I'm blessed not because of my righteousness but by the Righteousness of Jesus Christ.

2 CORINTHIANS 5:21
For He made Him who knew no sin to be sin for us, that we might become the righteousness of God in Him.

Jesus took my shame and past mistakes to the cross; hence, shame has no more claim on me and cannot shadow me any longer.

PSALM 31:1
In You, O Lord, I put my trust; Let me never be ashamed; Deliver me in Your righteousness.

The devil wants us to be under condemnation, but if our heart does not condemn us, we can have confidence in God and through God.

1 JOHN 3:21
Beloved, if our heart does not condemn us, we have confidence toward God.

For the wicked to keep us in shame and pain, our participation is always needed and is a matter of our will. So, reverse it. Withdraw the privilege from the accuser and refuse to be at the mercy of shame.

PSALM 119:78, 80
Let the proud be ashamed, For they treated me wrongfully with falsehood; But I will meditate on Your precepts. Let my heart be blameless regarding Your statutes, That I may not be ashamed.

When people feel shame and pressure, they want to run away. But running away is not the answer; it is total deliverance that's required.

The Deliverance

Hebrews 9:14
How much more shall the blood of Christ, who through the eternal Spirit offered Himself without spot to God, cleanse your conscience from dead works to serve the living God?

The BLOOD of Jesus Christ CLEAR & CLEANSES all the emotional pain & trauma.

My Confession

Say this out loud:

Thanks, Lord, for the blood.

Cleanse my mind,

Take away the pain,

Blot out all trauma and

Purge me with the Blood.

1 Thessalonians 2:13
For this reason we also thank God without ceasing, because when you received the word of God which you heard from us, you welcomed it not as the word of men, but as it is in truth, the word of God, which also effectively works in you who believe.

Receive the WORD and act on it. The word has supernatural powers to heal your mind, life, and emotions.

Declare the word with your mouth, for there is power in your tongue.

Proverbs 18:20-21
A man's stomach shall be satisfied from the fruit of his mouth; From the produce of his lips he shall be filled. Death and life are in the power of the tongue, And those who love it will eat its fruit.

My mouth determines what my life is filled with.

My words have spiritual powers and supernaturally :

RELEASE ANGELS

HEBREWS 1:14
Are they not all ministering spirits sent forth to minister for those who will inherit salvation?

RESTORES AUTHORITY

MATTHEW 18:18
Assuredly, I say to you, whatever you bind on earth will be bound in heaven, and whatever you loose on earth will be loosed in heaven.

RESTRICTS SPIRITUAL ADVERSARIES

JAMES 4:7
Therefore submit to God. Resist the devil and he will flee from you.

RESTRAINS ADVERSARIES

I PETER 5:9
Resist him, steadfast in the faith, knowing that the same sufferings are experienced by your brotherhood in the world.

RELEASES SPIRITUAL ACQUISITIONS

EPHESIANS 1:3
Blessed be the God and Father of our Lord Jesus Christ, who has blessed us with every spiritual blessing in the heavenly places in Christ.

ENABLES SPIRITUAL ACTIVITIES

REVELATION 12:11
And they overcame him by the blood of the Lamb and by the word of their testimony, and they did not love their lives to the death.

Every promise of the Bible is released by the word of your mouth.

ROMANS 10:9-10
That if you confess with your mouth the Lord Jesus and believe in your heart that God has raised Him from the dead, you will be saved. For with the

heart one believes unto righteousness, and with the mouth confession is made unto salvation.

Confess and say the word with discipline, especially what you want to happen in your life.

Every word of prophecy comes into manifestation and is enforced by what we say and confess with our MOUTH.

Mark 11:23-24
For assuredly, I say to you, whoever says to this mountain, 'Be removed and be cast into the sea,' and does not doubt in his heart, but believes that those things he says will be done, he will have whatever he says. Therefore I say to you, whatever things you ask when you pray, believe that you receive them, and you will have them.

Authority of Discouragement

Romans 5:17
For if by the one man's offence death reigned through the one, much more those who receive abundance of grace and of the gift of righteousness will reign in life through the One, Jesus Christ.)

Joshua 1:6-9
Be strong and of good courage, for to this people you shall divide as an inheritance the land which I swore to their fathers to give them. Only be strong and very courageous, that you may observe to do according to all the law which Moses My servant commanded you; do not turn from it to the right hand or to the left, that you may prosper wherever you go. This Book of the Law shall not depart from your mouth, but you shall meditate in it day and night, that you may observe to do according to all that is written in it. For then you will make your way prosperous, and then you will have good success. Have I not commanded you? Be strong and of good courage; do not be afraid, nor be dismayed, for the Lord your God is with you wherever you go.

1. Courage is always needed for success, lack of courage brings distress, non achievement.

2. Discouragement comes after waiting for a long time for a change that hadn't come.

3. Discouragement comes while expecting good news and a bad one comes

4. Looking over the errors of the past, affects our present and future and can lead to Discouragement.

To be discouraged MEANS:

- Process of abandoning hope because of UNMET EXPECTATIONS, UNWANTED PERSECUTION, UNREALISED POTENTIAL, UNEXPECTED BETRAYAL, UNRELENTED SETBACK
- An act of trying to make someone not do something
- To be low in spirit
- Develop cold feet
- Loss of confidence
- Feeling hopeless
- To be depressed and despair
- To be downcast and disappointed
- Suffer setback

For Example...

Our assignment or purpose in destiny is from the Lord and devil wants you to quit and be unfulfilled through weapon of DISCOURAGEMENT by stealing the vision.

In ACTS 16:9. Paul the apostle received a vision:

And a vision appeared to Paul in the night. A man of Macedonia stood and pleaded with him, saying, "Come over to Macedonia and help us.

Success is the proof that God spoke and gave the vision or assignment and it came to pass. We must take time to communicate vision clearly

HABAKKUK 2:2-3.
Then the Lord answered me and said: "Write the vision And make it plain on tablets, That he may run who reads it. For the vision is yet for an appointed time; But at the end it will speak, and it will not lie. Though it tarries, wait for it; Because it will surely come, It will not tarry."

Our divine assignment must also be defined and declared as with Jesus Christ in

LUKE 4:18.
The Spirit of the Lord is upon Me, Because He has anointed Me To preach the gospel to the poor; He has sent Me to heal the brokenhearted, To proclaim liberty to the captives And recovery of sight to the blind, To set at liberty those who are oppressed.

Our divine assignment must be talked about or discussed with our team so we can cooperate and corporately advance and work on the vision. But unfortunately divine assignment can be delayed because vision doesn't come to pass overnight.

Desire and dreams can be delayed, delay is not defeat.

HOW WE HANDLE DELAY HENCEFORTH REALLY MATTERS TO OUR DESTINY. DELIBERATELY CHOOSE TO BELIEVE THAT.

Every delay is working in your favour.

ROMANS 8:28.
And we know that all things work together for good to those who love God, to those who are the called according to His purpose.

When people cant wait for the vision to come to pass, they become DISCOURAGED and become DISTRACTED. Though vision tarries or lingers on, wait for it.

HABAKKUK 2:3.
For the vision is yet for an appointed time; But at the end it will speak, and it will not lie. Though it tarries, wait for it; Because it will surely come, It will not tarry.

Discouragement will stop the will to try and prevent us from moving forward.

Discouragement can overwrite the joy of past successes.

Discouragement always like to blame others but you must encourage yourself.

I Samuel 30:6
Now David was greatly distressed, for the people spoke of stoning him, because the soul of all the people was grieved, every man for his sons and his daughters. But David strengthened himself in the Lord his God.

Discouragement makes it hard to reach your goals, potential, destination or take possession of your situation

Moses got fed up and Elijah was fearful, they both experienced fear and discouragement.

Jesus was tempted to be discouraged.

Matthew 26:41
Watch and pray, lest you enter into temptation. The spirit indeed is willing, but the flesh is weak.

Paths to DISCOURAGEMENT

External Attacks

RIDICULE

REJECTION

REBELLION

THREATS FROM OTHERS

Internal Attacks

FEAR

FATIGUE

FRUSTRATION

How to Reign Over Discouragement

1. CHANGE YOUR PERSPECTIVE

Your way of thinking and seeing things, your mindset, attitude, viewpoint.

ROMANS 12:2.
And do not be conformed to this world, but be transformed by the renewing of your mind, that you may prove what is that good and acceptable and perfect will of God.

2. BE PRAYERFUL.

Prayer builds your confidence in God.

I JOHN 5:14
Now this is the confidence that we have in Him, that if we ask anything according to His will, He hears us.

Prayer draws you more to God.

JAMES 4:8
Draw near to God and He will draw near to you. Cleanse your hands, you sinners; and purify your hearts, you double-minded.

Prayer builds your faith in God.

JUDE 1:20
But you, beloved, building yourselves up on your most holy faith, praying in the Holy Spirit.

3. BEING PROACTIVE

Seeing the end from the beginning. Because the former plans were not working, to eliminate frustration, you need a new plan.

ISAIAH 43:18-19.
Do not remember the former things, Nor consider the things of old. Behold, I will do a new thing, Now it shall spring forth; Shall you not know it? I will even make a road in the wilderness And rivers in the desert.

Job 8:7
Though your beginning was small, Yet your latter end would increase abundantly.

4. FULLNESS OF PRAISE

Praise accelerates my efforts, ambushes and frustrates my enemies, accommodates my escape.

Paul and Silas Acts 16:25-26.

But at midnight Paul and Silas were praying and singing hymns to God, and the prisoners were listening to them. Suddenly there was a great earthquake, so that the foundations of the prison were shaken; and immediately all the doors were opened and everyone's chains were loosed.

2 Chronicles 20:22
Now when they began to sing and to praise, the Lord set ambushes against the people of Ammon, Moab, and Mount Seir, who had come against Judah; and they were defeated.

5. PERSEVERANCE

Spiritual determination never to quit or give up. Perseverance takes leverage away from the devil. My joy and hope and trust is in the Lord. Victory is mine and shall never give up.

Galatians 6:9
And let us not grow weary while doing good, for in due season we shall reap if we do not lose heart.

Hebrews 6:12
That you do not become sluggish, but imitate those who through faith and patience inherit the promises.

Authority Over Offences

Proverbs 18:19-21
A brother offended is harder to win than a strong city, And contentions are like the bars of a castle. A man's stomach shall be satisfied from the fruit of his

mouth; From the produce of his lips he shall be filled. Death and life are in the power of the tongue, And those who love it will eat its fruit

Authority

Delegated power to rule or manage God's determined plan and purposes.

Jesus took authority over:

1. Situations
2. Sickness and diseases
3. Satanic spirits
4. Demonic suggestions

Offences

- Wrongdoings, Violations, Displease
- Resentment, Indignation, Injustice
- Hurt, Outrage, A slap in the face
- Wounded feelings, To be out and down

Ways Offences come

1. Through PERCEIVED mistreatment against us.
2. By PROVEN malice against us (we must forgive and move on and not harbour resentment).
3. PERCEIVED mistreatment of others around us.
4. POINTLESS misguided expectations of others (when we expect too much from someone).
5. Unfounded and unreasonable PROFOUND reasons to be offended by fault finders (misguided thoughts against others).

Offences starts with demonic suggestions (fiery darts - **Ephesians 6:16**)

People offended are harbouring the hurts, resentments, bitterness etc on the inside.

When these thoughts are deposited, and if unchecked, it leads to people speaking about it.

Therefore thoughts are fuelled, rooted and anchored by spoken words.

Devil wants you Offended in order to destroy your meaningful relationships, Trusted relationship, Ministry association, Long time friendship, Family union, Business association, Marriages, GOD etc

When we're offended, it's hard to receive correction because PRIDE gets in the way.

Meaningful relationships are ORDAINED CHANNELS of Blessings such as:

– Ministry

– Family

– Partnership

– Church

– Friendship

– Business association

Our set place is our point of BLESSINGS. We need to therefore manage our relationship according to the word of God.

Offences hurts the offended more than one who created offence.

Matthew 5:23-24

Therefore if you bring your gift to the altar, and there remember that your brother has something against you, leave your gift there before the altar, and go your way. First be reconciled to your brother, and then come and offer your gift.

Overcoming Offences

1. Confront Offences to be able to get out of the entrapment and not be offended again.

MATTHEW 5:25
Agree with your adversary quickly, while you are on the way with him, lest your adversary deliver you to the judge, the judge hand you over to the officer, and you be thrown into prison.

2. Discuss and talk about the offence and deal with any issue.

2 TIMOTHY 2:23-24
But avoid foolish and ignorant disputes, knowing that they generate strife. And a servant of the Lord must not quarrel but be gentle to all, able to teach, patient.

3. Settle the matter and choose life, the way of peace.

DEUTERONOMY 30:19
I call heaven and earth as witnesses today against you, that I have set before you life and death, blessing and cursing; therefore choose life, that both you and your descendants may live.

4. Burry your pride and show humility. Calm down.

ROMANS 12:3
For I say, through the grace given to me, to everyone who is among you, not to think of himself more highly than he ought to think, but to think soberly, as God has dealt to each one a measure of faith.

5. Set the term for restoration even though it may be hard or tough and walk the path.

EPHESIANS 4:31-32
Let all bitterness, wrath, anger, clamor, and evil speaking be put away from you, with all malice. And be kind to one another, tenderhearted, forgiving one another, even as God in Christ forgave you.

6. Build pathway to trust back and restore relationship. Healing paths and amendments.

Titus 3:9
But avoid foolish disputes, genealogies, contentions, and strivings about the law; for they are unprofitable and useless.

Managing an Offended Relationship

If you're offended or you're in habit of causing offences, you need to be free.

We need to accept people the way they are, walk in agreement, and work hard to maintain good quality and long standing relationship. Don't let your pride get In the way.

Psalm 55:14
We took sweet counsel together, And walked to the house of God in the throng.

1. Decide and be honest with yourself that offence is POISONOUS and CAUSTIC.

Proverbs 27:3
A stone is heavy and sand is weighty, But a fool's wrath is heavier than both of them.

2. Be quick to repent and forgive and forget the offence.

James 1:19
So then, my beloved brethren, let every man be swift to hear, slow to speak, slow to wrath.

3. Saturate your mind with the word of God and give no room for the wicked.

Romans 12:1-2
I beseech you therefore, brethren, by the mercies of God, that you present your bodies a living sacrifice, holy, acceptable to God, which is your reasonable

service. And do not be conformed to this world, but be transformed by the renewing of your mind, that you may prove what is that good and acceptable and perfect will of God.

4. Confess the purifying power of the blood of Jesus.

Because hurts and pain may be deposited in offensive situation, we must purge our conscience of pain and memories associated with wrath and Offences.

HEBREWS 9:14
How much more shall the blood of Christ, who through the eternal Spirit offered Himself without spot to God, cleanse your conscience from dead works to serve the living God?

5. Eliminate all negative influences that can defile my thoughts. Close all doors and leave no room for the devil.

2 CORINTHIANS 10:5
Casting down arguments and every high thing that exalts itself against the knowledge of God, bringing every thought into captivity to the obedience of Christ.

6. Don't be condemned after forgiveness because of CIVIL consequences that may come. Court cases or prison.

ROMANS 9:33
As it is written: "Behold, I lay in Zion a stumbling stone and rock of offense, And whoever believes on Him will not be put to shame."

7. Establish a lifestyle of peace to exercise heart in Righteousness. Giving overflow of our LOVE of God to others.

HEBREWS 12:14-15
Pursue peace with all people, and holiness, without which no one will see the Lord: looking carefully lest anyone fall short of the grace of God; lest any root of bitterness springing up cause trouble, and by this many become defiled.

Resisting Offences

1. Realise the place of spiritual attack when harassed, or offended or people have done wrong against you.

Ephesians 6:12
For we do not wrestle against flesh and blood, but against principalities, against powers, against the rulers of the darkness of this age, against spiritual hosts of wickedness in the heavenly places.

2. Speak spiritual authority and truth to the Offence situation. Don't let what you say buy into the offence.

Titus 3:2
To speak evil of no one, to be peaceable, gentle, showing all humility to all men.

3 Resist the devil to stop the offence attacks. Lift up the shield of faith. Confrontation with spirit of darkness absolutely necessary.

Isaiah 59:19
So shall they fear The name of the Lord from the west, And His glory from the rising of the sun; When the enemy comes in like a flood, The Spirit of the Lord will lift up a standard against him.

4. Depend on God to help us with His word, Name and blood of Jesus. Weapons of enemy shall not prosper.

John 6:63
It is the Spirit who gives life; the flesh profits nothing. The words that I speak to you are spirit, and they are life.

Isaiah 54:17
No weapon formed against you shall prosper, And every tongue which rises against you in judgment You shall condemn. This is the heritage of the servants of the Lord, And their righteousness is from Me," Says the Lord.

5. Refuse to diminish and beat down yourself into low self esteem, Be Confident in God and walk in VICTORY. Supernatural power of God backs me up.

Philippians 1:28
And not in any way terrified by your adversaries, which is to them a proof of perdition, but to you of salvation, and that from God.

6. Keep confessing the word of the Lord because there's victory in your mouth.

Romans 10:10
For with the heart one believes unto righteousness, and with the mouth confession is made unto salvation.

7. Discover a whole new way of living in peace, love and joy. Get away from negative people and people that can cause you to stumble.

Psalm 119:165
Great peace have those who love Your law, And nothing causes them to stumble.

Chapter 11

CONFIDENT LIVING

Confident living

(Living free from demonic manipulation)

Ephesians 6:11-12
Finally, my brethren, be strong in the Lord and in the power of His might. Put on the whole armour of God, that you may be able to stand against the wiles of the devil.

There's a spiritual adversary.

1 Peter 5:8-9
Be sober, be vigilant; because your adversary the devil walks about like a roaring lion, seeking whom he may devour. Resist him, steadfast in the faith, knowing that the same sufferings are experienced by your brotherhood in the world.

When there's spiritual attack, I need to fight back (resist).

Fight with the devil must end when I resist him.

Ephesians 6:16
Above all, taking the shield of faith with which you will be able to quench all the fiery darts of the wicked one.

Resist the devil:

Fiery darts are demonic thoughts in my mind that wants to talk me out of the scripture and God's love and care to make me have a pessimistic view and thought of myself; situations and other people. Thereby stealing my joy and peace.

2 CORINTHIANS 2:11 – not take advantage of us.

The devil attacks us as he intends to cause:

- Discouragement
- Discontentment
- Distress
- Devalue
- Destruction (suicide)

My kingdom value to be victorious henceforth is based on:

a) Price Christ paid

b) Possession of whom (God) I am

c) Potential I have

1 JOHN 3:21
Beloved, if our heart does not condemn us, we have confidence toward God.

Devil is looking for self-indictment of shame – wants me to devalue myself through condemnation.

If your heart does not condemn you, then have confidence in God.

When my heart is condemning me, I start talking negative from my heart, not seeing possibilities, talking about bad situations etc.

But as I keep working on my heart and developing myself spiritually, my confidence in God increases and my victory is assured.

Attack of the devil is to affect my:

TIMING (so I hesitate when making important decisions)

THINKING – wants me to have impossibility thinking rather than favour thinking.

TONGUE – wants me to buy into pessimistic (negative) talks rather than possibilities.

TEMPERAMENT – wants me to walk around pitiful so that people feel sorry for me.

JAMES 1:2
My brethren, count it all joy when you fall into various trials.

ROMANS 8:28
And we know that all things work together for good to those who love God, to those who are the called according to His purpose.

Divine moment of the Father, because God is speaking to you, had arrested you and infusing a new thought into you (what He is able to do). New Possibilities.

The devil can't steal my joy because of what I know, my future, power of God, Holy Spirit, God's plan and His love for me.

For things I don't know, I trust and believe God for. But for what I know, I press in for my victory and trust Him more.

My change comes from God increasing in me because it's about His grace, goodness and mercies.

My confidence is in Him, through His – ability and authority.

Moses at the red sea, Gideon and little army, Widow of Zarephath.

Taking Bold Steps for Confident Living

ROMANS 10:11
For the Scripture says, "Whoever believes on Him will not be put to shame.

Psalm 31:1
In You, O Lord, I put my trust; Let me never be ashamed; Deliver me in Your righteousness.

Humiliating, demoralising pain in our heart is a product or experience of shame.

When I take what brings shame upon myself, it makes me to be ashamed. Shame short circuits us and makes us to miss the best and the plans of God.

The fear in shame doesn't allow us to make brilliant decision in our lives. Shame prevents us from living a confident life.

Ephesians 5:11, 12, 16
And have no fellowship with the unfruitful works of darkness, but rather expose them. For it is shameful even to speak of those things which are done by them in secret... redeeming the time, because the days are evil.

Recognise spiritual attack as the devil is working to derail, disqualify and disdain us.

Our choices are vitally important because we live or die by the choices we make.

When we make decision based on humiliation, shame, negativity, we won't be bold enough to make quality decision.

Isaiah 1:!9
If you are willing and obedient, You shall eat the good of the land.

A point where we choose to trust God and leave worry behind and take a bold step (through being willing and obedient to the Lord) becomes our defining or divine moment.

Divine Moment in Confident Living

A time when I need to make a choice when prompted by the Spirit of God.

- Moses experience at the burning bush was a moment of providence because God arranged it.
- David fighting Goliath was also arranged by God.
- Gideon's assignment was also orchestrated by God.

A divine moment can also be a moment of PRAYER where we get intuition or witness from the Lord.

- Church was praying when Peter was freed from prison, hence had boldness to obey. Angel was dispatched to Peter.
- Nehemiah succeeded because he prayed and also had a strong witness to build the wall.

Divine moment can also be a moment of proclamation when preaching of the word enables your spirit within you to hear from the Lord through inward witness.

Faith comes from hearing from the Lord. ROMANS 10:17

Divine moment are also moments of God's PURSUIT.

ROMANS 15:4 – have hope through comfort of scriptures.

Many heard and trust what God said.

Shunamite woman – built penthouse for Elisha. 2 KINGS 4:10

- Shirophenician woman – believed Jesus for healing of her daughter. MARK 7:26-30
- Zarephath widow – obeyed by giving to prophet and had prosperity. *1 Kings 17*

Divine Moments and Myself

I have to respect DIVINE ALIGNMENT (God had set some things in order and I have to believe that things will fall into place). Trust God and believe for change. God already knows what He is going to do.

I must expect that DEMONIC ARGUMENTS must come and must be expelled. PSALM 23:5

Devil comes to keep me worried through:

- REASONING arguments – comes to belittle us and speak impossibilities.

- REPUTATION arguments – comes to say if failure comes, it will wreck our reputation. People hesitate based on fear of failure.

- RELIABILITY arguments – enemy comes with fiery darts of doubt to question God's commitment. Cast down all thoughts and arguments 2 Corinthians 10:4-5.

- RESOURCE arguments – questioning supply sources (where will I get help, people, money etc). Insufficiency of time, team and treasure must shift from us to God as God increases in us to honour His words in our lives. My dependence is based on God, not my skills, talents or gifts. Proverbs 3:5-6. We must discipline ourselves to let God increase in our lives so that all burdens can be put or cast on the Lord. 1 Peter 5:7

- RIGHTEOUS arguments – the enemy wants to disqualify us based on what we did. When he tricks us into believing that grace was not sufficient, we back away and give up. My mistake does not cancel God's goodness and mercy toward me. Mercy is when I don't get what I deserve based on my wrongdoing. Mercy says because you asked for forgiveness, God wiped the slate clean and we are blessed all the way.

Discipline for Confident Living

Obeying God – is a priority because He is my helper.

PSALM 121 – His acceptance must be a necessity

We must take bold action even when we don't understand what to do.

(information from God is a need to know basis). We must have what we need when it's needed and must have it because of Him as our supplier.

We must address everything contrary to the word. Cast down imaginations and appropriate words of our mouth. Confess with your mouth to salvation. Get victory with your mouth. No matter where we are, we must trust the Lord as our FATHER because God is concerned about us. When we repent, God accelerates His mercy to us. Luke 15 (prodigal son).

JAMES 4:7 – resist the devil and negative thoughts.

Confident living is pursuing abundant living with bold assurance in the love of God for His:

Protection, Provision and Promises.

Confident living is trusting the Lord through a disciplined lifestyle.

Discipline is enforced obedience where we live beyond feelings and desire to have purposeful result.

JOHN 8:31-32 – continue in the word as a disciple.

Then Jesus said to those Jews who believed Him, "If you abide in My word, you are My disciples indeed. And you shall know the truth, and the truth shall make you free."

Focus and develop discipline.

Discipline is a lifestyle not being ruled by feelings and circumstances.

ROMANS 10:9
That if you confess with your mouth the Lord Jesus and believe in your heart that God has raised Him from the dead, you will be saved.

Dynamics of Jesus Commitment Through His Lordship.

Jesus has the right to tell me what to do and direct my life through my relationship with my Lord and Saviour.

Through His Lordship I have received:

Redemption. He paid the price for my sins.

Righteousness. Right standing with God and all benefits of right standing with God is mine and I have been made righteous. My righteousness is not based on PERFORMANCE but on position.

2 Corinthians 5:20-21. Place in right standing with God.

Romans 5:17. Gift of righteousness was given to me when Jesus took away my sin.

Psalm 31:1. My deliverance is based on His righteousness.

Psalm 5:12. I am Favoured for life

Psalm 34:19. Deliverance from all affliction

Relationship. Now I'm a child of God.

John 1:12. Power to be child of God

Galatians 3:26. Child of God through Jesus Christ.

Sovereign Call to Confident Living:

CALL TO PURPOSE: my purpose in life is a part of my good works. Ephesians 2:10 we are God's workmanship to do good works and fulfilment.

CALL TO PARTNERSHIP: Ephesians 4:1. Every vision from the Lord is pre-programmed that others may be blessed.

CALL TO A PLACE: 1 Corinthians 12:18. The place we go (to worship) is important. Being on the spot and staying in our set place so that all God ordained for us can come to pass. We must not be DISPLEASED so as not to be DISPLACED from our set place of blessing.

Be disciplined by one word from the Lord not to be moved by the fiery darts of the enemy.

My breakthrough or confident living comes when I trust God.

I trust God in all ways by His:

Personal REFERENCE

Perfected RELATIONSHIP

Process REGIMENT. His process of working.

Proven RESULT (proof of what He has done).

Milton Keynes UK
Ingram Content Group UK Ltd.
UKHW050859091124
450781UK00013B/132